# How to Use
# AMERICA ONLINE

# How to Use
# AMERICA
# ONLINE

## CHRISTOPHER J. BENZ

Illustrated by
SARAH ISHIDA

**Ziff-Davis Press**
**Emeryville, California**

| | |
|---|---|
| Copy Editor | Carol Henry |
| Technical Reviewer | Maryann Brown |
| Project Coordinators | Barbara Dahl and Cort Day |
| Proofreader | Carol Burbo |
| Cover Illustration | Regan Honda |
| Cover Design | Regan Honda and Carrie English |
| Book Design | Dennis Gallagher/Visual Strategies, San Francisco |
| Screen Graphics Editor | Dan Brodnitz |
| Technical Illustration | Sarah Ishida |
| Word Processing | Howard Blechman |
| Page Layout | M.D. Barrera |
| Indexer | Carol Burbo |

Ziff-Davis Press books are produced on a Macintosh computer system with the following applications: FrameMaker®, Microsoft® Word, QuarkXPress®, Adobe Illustrator®, Adobe Photoshop®, Adobe Streamline™, MacLink® *Plus*, Aldus® FreeHand™, Collage Plus™.

If you have comments or questions or would like to receive a free catalog, call or write:
Ziff-Davis Press
5903 Christie Avenue
Emeryville, CA 94608
1-800-688-0448

ISBN 1-56276-258-3

Manufactured in the United States of America
⊕ This book is printed on paper that contains 50% total recycled fiber of which 20% is de-inked postconsumer fiber.
10 9 8 7 6 5 4 3 2

# TABLE OF CONTENTS

# ACKNOWLEDGMENTS

 Learning guides such as this one depend on the smooth flow of ideas and the consistent, correct use of language. Copy editor and part-time counselor Carol Henry deserves hearty praise for simultaneously massaging my words, my ego, and my funny bone. Other invaluable members of the word team were series editor Kim Haglund, technical reviewer Maryann Brown, project coordinators Cort Day and Barbara Dahl, and proofreader and indexer Carol Burbo.

A quick flip through this book will show that the book is at least as much about graphics as it is about words. Graphical wizardry kudos go to illustrator Sarah Ishida, designer Dennis Gallagher, layout artist M.D. Barrera, and the intrepid screen-shot expert Dan Brodnitz.

Thanks also to the many other professionals who contributed in some way to the process of creating this book. At America Online: Marshall Rens, Pam McGraw, Henry "Hal" Rosengarten, Mark Hulme, Diane Johnson, Mark Miller, Tim Barwick, Margaret Ryan, and everyone whose screen name begins with "Advisor" or "TECHLive." At Ziff-Davis Press: Eric Stone, Cheryl Holzaepfel, Cindy Hudson, Cori Pansarasa, Howard Blechman, Pipi Diamond, and everyone in the Accounting Department.

Finally, my sincerest thanks go to my wife, Kat, who's always there when I need her.

# INTRODUCTION

 You're new to America Online and its companion communications program, America Online for Windows. Maybe you're not quite sure what an online service is or what a communications program does. Maybe you've never even used a computer before. You're not looking to become an expert. You don't need hotshot shortcuts. You just want to see how this online thing works.

*How to Use America Online* is for you. This concise, colorful book takes you on a guided tour, during which you'll see how to tap into America Online's many treasures—right before your eyes, step by step, topic by topic. When you're done reading this book, you'll be a comfortable, confident America Online member. From games and electronic mail to online news and the legendary Internet, the power and fun of online information will be right at your fingertips.

Each chapter in this book presents up to five related topics. Because each topic fits in a section spanning just two facing pages, everything you need to know about that topic is in front of you at one time. Just follow the numbered steps around the pages, reading the text and looking at the pictures. It's really as easy as it looks!

Colorful, realistic examples are included to help you understand your options for using America Online. You can work along as you learn, but that's not at all mandatory. If you want to stay focused on your own information needs and use this book just as a reference, you'll find it well suited to that purpose.

Even experienced computer users occasionally stumble into unfamiliar territory. Read the "Tip Sheet" accompanying each topic to learn more about related pitfalls or about alternative methods for accomplishing the task at hand.

You also will find two special sections called "Try It!" at strategic spots in this book. Each Try It! section is a hands-on exercise that gives you valuable practice with some of the skills you've acquired to that point. As you read a Try It! section, be sure to follow each step at your computer.

To get the most value out of this book, read the topics in sequence. If you already have some experience with America Online, or with online services and computers in general, you may be familiar with the information in the first two chapters. Skimming these chapters, however, can provide a useful refresher on major concepts and terminology.

I am eager to know your reactions to this book. Please mail any comments and suggestions for future editions to

Christopher J. Benz
Ziff-Davis Press
5903 Christie Avenue
Emeryville, CA 94608
Electronic mail: 6229438@mcimail.com

Have a good trip!

**Note:** This book was specifically designed for use with version 1.5 of the America Online for Windows communications software, but works almost equally as well with version 1.1. Version 1.1 users should notice only a few minor differences between how their software works and how it is described within.

# CHAPTER 1

# What Is an Online Service?

An *online service*, from a technical point of view, is a commercial telecommunications system that provides a way for your computer to connect to other computers for the purpose of exchanging information. It's a *telecommunications system* because you communicate with the service by means of ordinary telephone lines. It's a *commercial service* because you pay money so that the service provider can make a profit.

From a more personal aspect, an online service is the world at your fingertips. With an online service, you can get the latest news and weather reports, check out how your favorite sports team did last night, read a couple of jokes, send a message to a friend halfway around the world, order a pair of plane tickets, and ask a complete stranger for advice—all without getting up from your computer.

This book teaches you how to use one online service, America Online, which is widely regarded as one of the most graphical and easiest to use services around. Read on to find out why.

# America Online Is Your Online Service

**A**merica Online isn't the only online service available. Just as different banks serve the various financial needs of any community, there are more than a few online services to serve the information needs of the nation and the world. As with banks, all online services offer the same basic features, but each does so with a unique emphasis. Services such as CompuServe focus on the needs of businesses and experienced computer users. Others, America Online included, tend to serve more personal needs. This isn't to say that you can't use CompuServe to meet some personal needs, or America Online to address business issues— it's simply a matter of focus.

## TIP SHEET

▶ **This book is about using the America Online for Windows version 1.1 or version 1.5 software to connect to the America Online service. Unless you have the right software, you cannot be sure that everything you read in this book applies to you. Look on your America Online installation disk(s) for the number *1.1* or *1.5* and the phrase *for Windows*; if you find you have the wrong disk(s), call America Online (1-800-827-6364) and ask for a free replacement.**

▶ **Your modem may be internal, hidden inside your computer's main case, or external, a small box sitting outside the case. If you're not sure whether you have a modem, check with the vendor who sold you your computer, or ask a computer-savvy friend.**

▶ **Chapter 2 of this book is for first-time computer users or first-time Windows users. If you can start Windows, use your mouse, issue menu commands, and select dialog box options, you can skip ahead to Chapter 3. If you don't know what these operations are, or if you need to review them, then Chapter 2 is just for you.**

**America Online, Inc.**

**Welcome**

▶ **1** America Online consists of two basic components: the *service* and the *communications software*. To keep things straight, we'll refer to the service, or the service and software collectively, as *America Online*. When we talk specifically about the software, we'll say *America Online for Windows*. (More about Windows in a moment.)

**7** What makes America Online so popular? Well, it's easy to learn, easy to use, relatively fast, and supplies information from many different arenas. As a new user, you'll appreciate the ease of use; as you work with America Online more and more, you'll come to appreciate its speed and diversity.

**6** America Online is well regarded by many computer users. You'll be using an online service and communications software that have withstood the test of time and acquired hundreds of thousands of faithful members.

**2** America Online, the service, is headquartered in Vienna, Virginia (a suburb of Arlington, just outside Washington, D.C.). It's a set of computers—collectively known as *The Stratus* by people who like to name computers—that contains loads of information ready for the taking. This information is constantly updated so that when you check something such as a news report, you can be sure that you're getting the most recent information.

**3** America Online for Windows, the software, resides on the hard disks of computers that are set up to connect to America Online. Just as a CD player needs CDs to make music, each computer needs software to tell it what to do. America Online for Windows tells your computer how to connect to America Online. (Computers can be set up to run all types of software, including word processors, spreadsheets, databases, and games.) You'll learn how to set up America Online for Windows on your computer in Chapter 3.

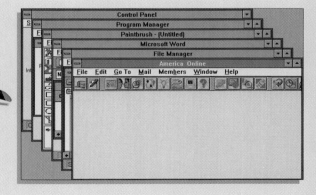

**4** As the name implies, America Online for Windows is software that is based on *Microsoft Windows*, a program that controls, among other things, the "look" of your computer screen. The America Online for Windows *interface* (that is, the way you give commands to the software and receive information from it) is similar to that of other Windows-based software, including some you may already know how to use. (More about Windows in Chapter 2.)

**5** To make the connection between your computer and the ones in Virginia, you use ordinary telephone lines. Because telephone lines are designed for human voices rather than computer information, your computer must have a special piece of equipment called a *modem* (short for *modulator/demodulator*) to translate the computer information traveling to and from your computer.

**CHAPTER 2**

# Getting Acquainted with DOS and Windows

 DOS and Windows are programs (the terms *program* and *software* are used interchangeably here) that enable you to run the programs you really *want* to run: your communications software (America Online for Windows), your word processor, your games, and so on.

DOS, short for *disk operating system*, copies information to and from the disks in your computer. Without an operating system, your computer cannot do anything useful (except, perhaps, be a step stool). You can't run software such as America Online for Windows unless you first tell DOS to copy the software from a disk into *random access memory* (RAM), a temporary holding place inside your computer. Likewise, you cannot store and later reuse information that you receive from America Online unless you have DOS copy it from RAM onto a disk.

Windows can simplify your role in directing these and many other computer affairs. It also provides a consistent and fairly appealing backdrop for all *Windows-based software*. Windows-based programs look comfortingly similar on the screen, and there are many similarities in the way you work with these programs.

You don't need to start DOS manually; it starts automatically whenever you turn on your computer. Windows, on the other hand, is an add-on program that may or may not start automatically. However, Windows *must* be started before you can use America Online for Windows. This chapter helps you start and use Windows.

# How to Start Windows from DOS

The heart and soul of DOS, at least from your viewpoint, is the *DOS prompt*. The DOS prompt provides you an opportunity to ask DOS to do something. By typing *commands* at this prompt, you can run programs, check the contents of your disks, reset the time and date on your computer's internal clock, and much more. For now, the only DOS command you absolutely must know is the one to start Windows.

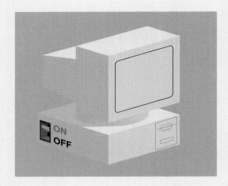

▶ **1** Switch on your computer. You may need to flick switches on several components of your computer system, including the main case containing the hard disk and floppy-disk drives, the monitor (screen), the modem (if it's an external modem), and the printer. Give the computer a minute or so to go through its wake-up ritual. When it's ready to accept information from you, it will ask you for specific information or it will display the DOS prompt.

▶ **Your computer may be set up to bypass the DOS prompt and start Windows automatically. If Windows has started, you'll probably see the words "Program Manager" somewhere on the screen. In this case, you can skip steps 4 and 5.**

▶ **Some computers automatically start *DOS Shell*, a program designed to help you enter commands without using the DOS prompt. If DOS Shell is running, you'll see the words "MS-DOS Shell" at the top of your screen. To return to the DOS prompt, hold down the Alt key, press and release the F4 function key (located on the left side or top row of your keyboard), and then release Alt.**

▶ **Your computer may display a *custom menu* in place of, or in addition to, the DOS prompt. If this menu contains a selection for Windows, use the menu to start Windows. If the menu does not contain any such entry, consult the person who set up the menu.**

**5** If the preceding step produced an error message such as "Bad command or file name," try typing **c:\windows\win** and then pressing Enter. Still can't start Windows? Well, the possible reasons and solutions are too many to enumerate here, but a computer-savvy friend or family member should be able to help you in short order. You can also call Microsoft technical support (the telephone number is in your Windows manual), which routinely helps solve such problems.

2 Type in any information the computer requests; for example, some computers ask for the date and time. Then press the Enter key.

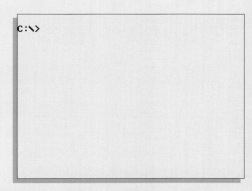

```
C:\>
```

3 After you've provided any initial information your computer needs, you'll see the DOS prompt. This is how DOS lets you know that it's ready to accept commands. The most common DOS prompt looks like C:\>, but it can vary. For example, the prompt may be gussied up with special characters such as brackets, it may display the current date or time, or it may even appear as a message, such as "Type in a command, please." No matter how your DOS prompt looks, you'll start Windows the same way.

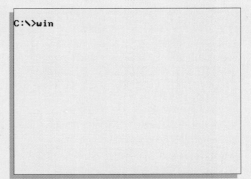

```
C:\>win
```

4 Type **win**, and then press Enter. This command starts Windows on most computers. After a few seconds, you'll see the words "Program Manager" somewhere on the screen, indicating that Windows is now running. If this happens, you can skip the next step.

# How to Start a Program from Program Manager

**P**rogram Manager is a Windows-based program that serves as the command center for Windows. Its role is to make it easy for you to start *other* programs from within Windows. Program Manager opens automatically when you start Windows, and remains open as long as Windows is running. This picture shows how Program Manager might look when you start Windows. Then again, Windows is highly customizable, so your starting screen may look quite different.

▶ **1** A *window* is simply an on-screen box containing information. Like most Windows-based programs, Program Manager has an *application window* and multiple *document windows*. Every window contains a *title bar*, which displays the name of the program or document in that window. In this screen, six windows are wholly or partially visible. Solitaire, America Online for Windows, Program Manager, and Calculator are application windows. Welcome and Accessories are document windows.

**Control Menu boxes**

**Application window**

**Document window**

**TIP SHEET**

▶ **To close an application or document window, double-click on the *Control Menu box* in that window's upper-left corner (or click once on the box and then click on Close). Closing the Program Manager application window closes Windows and returns you to the DOS prompt, or to wherever you were when you first started Windows.**

▶ **To open a program group window using the keyboard, hold down the Alt key and type w to open the Window menu, release Alt, and then type the number that appears next to the program group you want to open. This technique is especially useful if the desired program group is hidden behind other program groups.**

▶ **To start a program using the keyboard, open its program group window, use the arrow keys to highlight the program item, and then press Enter.**

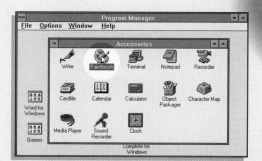

**6** To then start a program such as Paintbrush within the Accessories group, locate its program item in the program group window, point to the program item icon, and double-click.

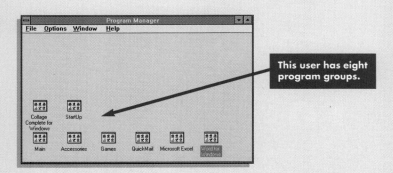

This user has eight program groups.

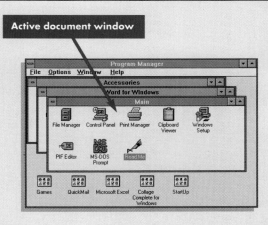

Active document window

**2** You issue commands from an application window's *menu bar*, under the title bar. The application window for Program Manager also contains *icons* (small pictures) representing *program groups*. Program groups are document windows that contain other icons representing related collections of programs.

**3** You can have zero, one, or multiple document windows open at one time, but only one document window can be active. The *active document window* is the one that will be affected by commands you issue. The title bar of the active document window appears in a different color or shade than the title bars of inactive document windows.

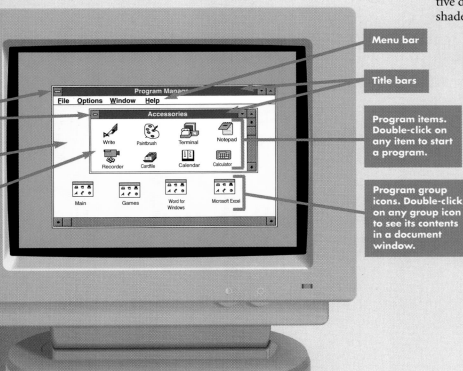

Menu bar

Title bars

Program items. Double-click on any item to start a program.

Program group icons. Double-click on any group icon to see its contents in a document window.

This Accessories program group contains 13 program items.

**4** Document windows often contain actual documents. In Program Manager, however, document windows contain *program items*, icons that represent computer programs. The fact that the window is called a "document window" is a quirk of Windows terminology. For clarity, many people refer to document windows in Program Manager as *program group windows*.

**5** So how do all these elements work together? When you want to start a program, first open the program group that contains the desired program item. For instance, to open the Accessories program group, move the mouse until the on-screen arrow points to the Accessories icon, and then *double-click* (click the left mouse button twice in rapid succession).

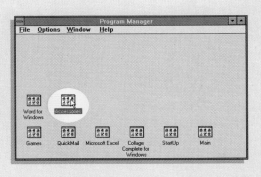

# How to Use the Mouse in Windows

**A**n *input device* is a means of giving instructions to your computer. You may be familiar with the keyboard as the most common input device. (If not, don't worry; we'll cover that next.) A *mouse*, so named for its size and tail-like cable, is a hand-held input device that, along with the keyboard, is one of the two input devices typically used in Windows. Although it's possible to get by without a mouse and instead do everything from the keyboard, it's not recommended. Windows and Windows-based programs were designed with the mouse in mind. Keyboard alternatives can be awkward—and it's not always easy to find out what those alternatives are. Take a few minutes to learn the major mouse techniques, and your efforts will pay off handsomely.

## TIP SHEET

▶ It takes some practice to become efficient with a mouse, especially when double-clicking and dragging. Be patient; you'll feel like an expert in no time.

▶ Some mice have two buttons, and others have three. The right mouse button is used infrequently, and the middle mouse button is almost never used unless you have a special mouse program to take advantage of it.

▶ Unless you're told otherwise, always use the *left* mouse button. The other mouse buttons are used so infrequently in Windows that when they *are* needed, you'll always be told about it specifically.

▶ Mice are not the only pointing devices available. If your computer is equipped with some other type of pointing device, such as a trackball or pointing stick, you can use that instead of a mouse.

▶ **1** Grab your mouse with the "tail" pointing away from you and your fingers resting over the buttons, and then move the mouse around on your mouse pad or desktop. As you do, the on-screen *mouse pointer* moves in synch with the mouse. Usually, the mouse pointer appears as either an arrow or an I-beam. Because you use the mouse to point, mice are sometimes called *pointing devices.*

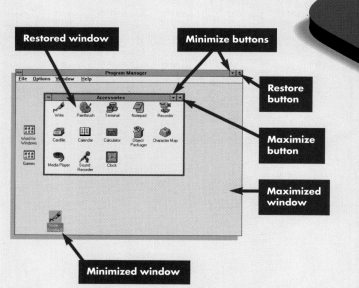

**6** To *maximize* a window (that is, to enlarge it so that an application window fills the screen or a document window fills its application window), click on the window's *Maximize button.* To *restore* a maximized window to its previous size, click on the window's *Restore button* (which will appear in place of the Maximize button). To *minimize* a window to just an icon, click on the window's *Minimize button.* To restore a minimized window to its previous size, double-click on the icon (or click once on the icon, and then click on Restore).

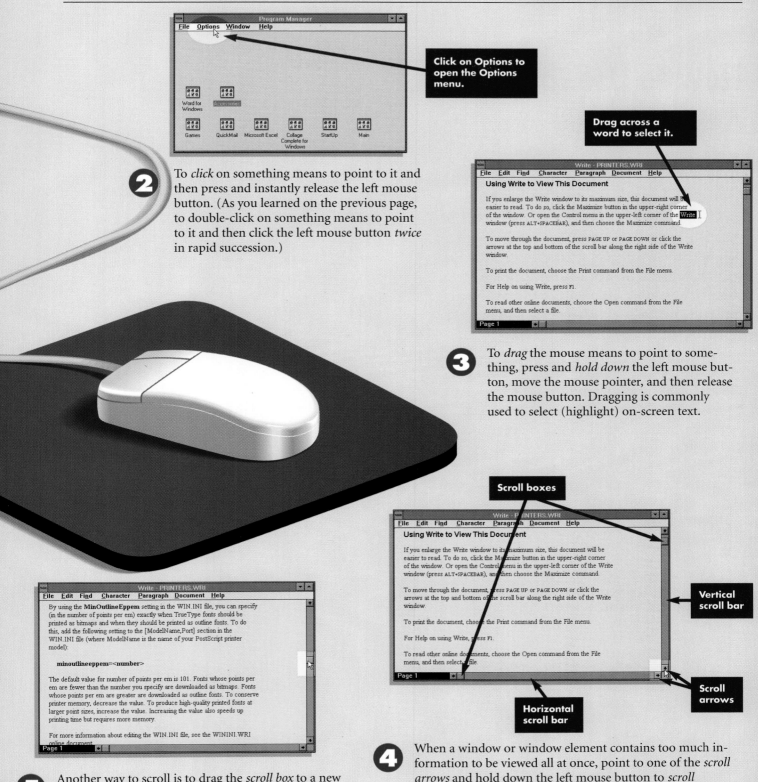

**Click on Options to open the Options menu.**

**Drag across a word to select it.**

**2** To *click* on something means to point to it and then press and instantly release the left mouse button. (As you learned on the previous page, to double-click on something means to point to it and then click the left mouse button *twice* in rapid succession.)

**3** To *drag* the mouse means to point to something, press and *hold down* the left mouse button, move the mouse pointer, and then release the mouse button. Dragging is commonly used to select (highlight) on-screen text.

**Scroll boxes**

**Vertical scroll bar**

**Horizontal scroll bar**

**Scroll arrows**

**4** When a window or window element contains too much information to be viewed all at once, point to one of the *scroll arrows* and hold down the left mouse button to *scroll* through the display in the direction of the arrow.

**5** Another way to scroll is to drag the *scroll box* to a new location on the *scroll bar*. The position of the scroll box suggests what part of the window's contents you are viewing. For example, when the scroll box is in about the middle of the vertical scroll bar, you are about halfway down from the top of the window contents.

# How to Use the Keyboard in Windows

In Windows and most Windows-based programs, you don't have to use the keyboard for much of anything—except, of course, to type text. But if you do quite a bit of typing, you may be interested in optional ways to scroll through windows, issue commands, and perform other common actions *without* having to reach for the mouse. The more you work with Windows, the more you may yearn for keyboard alternatives to mouse actions that seem inconvenient to you. Even if you're a true "mouse-o-phile," you should be aware of the major keyboard techniques in case your mouse ever malfunctions.

**TIP SHEET**

▶ In many programs, the Page Up and Page Down keys (sometimes labeled PgUp and PgDn) scroll the window in large increments. Ctrl+Home often moves you to the beginning of a window's contents, and Ctrl+End often moves you to the end.

▶ Your keyboard may not look exactly like the one pictured here, especially if your keyboard is a few years old or if you're using a small, portable computer. All keyboards, however, share essentially the same set of keys. If you have trouble finding the keys described here, check the documentation that came with your computer.

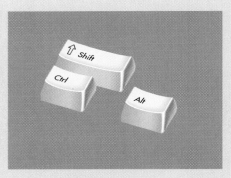

▶ **1** The Shift, Alt, and Ctrl keys almost always work in combination with other keys. You probably know that holding down the Shift key as you press a letter key produces a capital letter. The Alt and Ctrl keys work the same way, but the results depend on the program you are using at the time.

**7** The Escape key (labeled Esc on most keyboards) lets you back out of many potentially hazardous situations. If you open a menu, but decide not to issue a command, press Escape twice to close the menu and deactivate the menu bar. If you issue a command and a dialog box opens, but you don't want to proceed, press Escape once to close the dialog box. (Dialog boxes are described on the next page.)

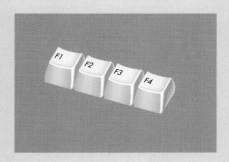

**2** The Shift, Alt, and Ctrl keys are often combined with the *function keys*—labeled F1 through F10, F12, or F16—to issue commands. For example, you can close most Windows programs by pressing Alt+F4 (hold down Alt, press and release F4, and then release Alt). The function keys can also work alone. The function keys are usually located in the keyboard's top row (as shown here) or along the keyboard's left side.

**3** When you don't want to reach for the mouse to scroll through the contents of a window, use the ↑, ↓, ←, and → *arrow keys* instead. Many keyboards contain *two* sets of arrow keys. Arrow keys that display just arrows always work as arrow keys. Arrow keys that display both arrows and numbers, however, are dual-purpose keys; they can work as arrow keys *or* as number keys. To toggle these dual-purpose keys, use the Num Lock key.

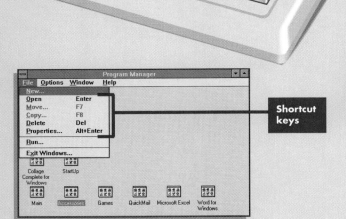

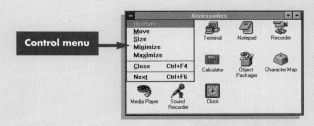

Control menu

**4** Another way to maximize, minimize, restore, or close a window is through its Control menu. Press Alt+Spacebar to open an application window's Control menu; press Alt+hyphen to open a document window's Control menu. Use the ↓ key to highlight the command you want: Maximize, Minimize, Restore, or Close. Then press Enter.

Shortcut keys

Type the underlined character to select the menu item and issue the command.

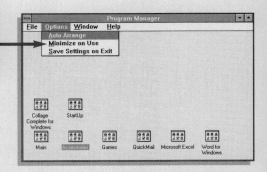

**6** Many menus also list keyboard alternatives (shortcut keys) right next to their most frequently used commands. Although these shortcut keys work only when the menu is closed, the listing serves as a reminder for next time.

**5** To open a menu from the menu bar, hold down Alt, type the underlined character in the menu name (for example, F for File or O for Options), and then release Alt. To select an item from an open menu, use the ↓ and Enter keys as described in step 4, or simply type the item's underlined character.

# How to Talk to a Dialog Box

**A** *dialog box* is basically an on-screen questionnaire where you provide the extra information a program needs to carry out a command you have issued. For example, say you issue the File, Print command, which is available in many Windows-based programs. Before printing anything, however, the program will open a dialog box to ask you how much of the current window contents to print, how many copies to print, what printer to use, and so on. Once you answer these questions, the command is executed.

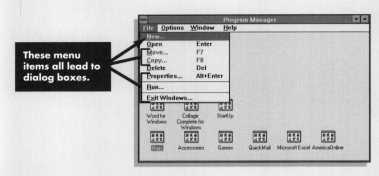

These menu items all lead to dialog boxes.

**▶ ❶** An ellipsis (…) after a menu item indicates that clicking on that item will open a dialog box.

Radio buttons

OK

**❼** When you've provided all the requested information in a dialog box, click on the *OK button*, or on another of the available *command buttons*. (The button names will be Print, Find, or something else related to the command.)

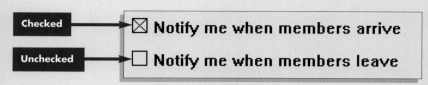

**Checked**

**Unchecked**

☒ Notify me when members arrive

☐ Notify me when members leave

**2** One way to answer a dialog-box question is to check or uncheck a *check box*. Click in an empty check box to check it; an X fills the box to show that the option is active. Click in a checked check box to turn off the option; the X disappears.

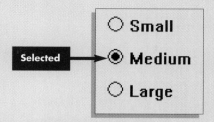

**Selected**

○ Small
◉ Medium
○ Large

**3** Sometimes dialog-box options are grouped as *radio buttons* (also known as *option buttons*). You can select (activate) only one radio button within a group at one time, and at least one button must be selected at all times. Select a radio button by clicking on it; the previously selected button automatically clears. It works just like the station-selector buttons on old-style car radios—hence the name.

**Text boxes**

**Command buttons**

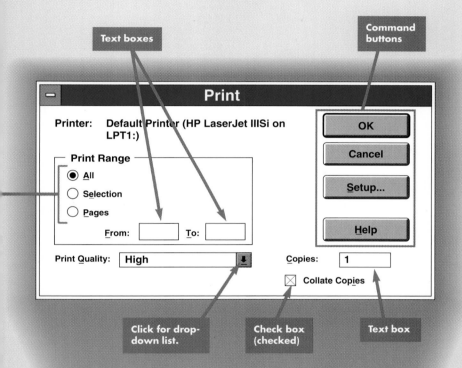

**Print**

Printer:   Default Printer (HP LaserJet IIISi on LPT1:)

**Print Range**
◉ All
○ Selection
○ Pages

From: [    ]   To: [    ]

Print Quality: [ High            ▼ ]

Copies: [ 1 ]

☒ Collate Copies

[ OK ]
[ Cancel ]
[ Setup... ]
[ Help ]

**Click for drop-down list.**

**Check box (checked)**

**Text box**

**Click on the desired item.**

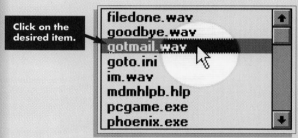

filedone.wav
goodbye.wav
gotmail.wav
goto.ini
im.wav
mdmhlpb.hlp
pcgame.exe
phoenix.exe

**4** A *list box* displays a list of choices. Generally, you can select only one choice. If your choice isn't visible, use the list box's scroll bar to scroll through the list.

**Click here to scroll down through the drop-down list.**

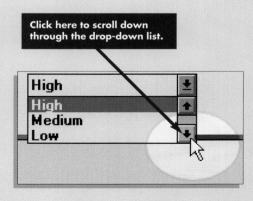

High
High
Medium
Low

**Text boxes**

**Click, and then type.**

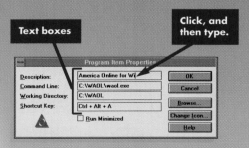

Program Item Properties

Description:        America Online for W
Command Line:       C:\WAOL\waol.exe
Working Directory:  C:\WAOL
Shortcut Key:       Ctrl + Alt + A

☐ Run Minimized

[ OK ]
[ Cancel ]
[ Browse... ]
[ Change Icon... ]
[ Help ]

**6** To enter or change text in a *text box*, first click anywhere in the box. Then use the arrow keys to position the *insertion point* (the flashing vertical bar), use the Backspace and Delete keys to delete the existing text as needed, and then type new text from the keyboard.

**5** A down-pointing arrow with a line below it means you can click on the arrow to see a *drop-down list* of choices. When you spot your choice, click on it. If your choice isn't visible, use the list's scroll bar.

## CHAPTER 3

# Welcome to America Online

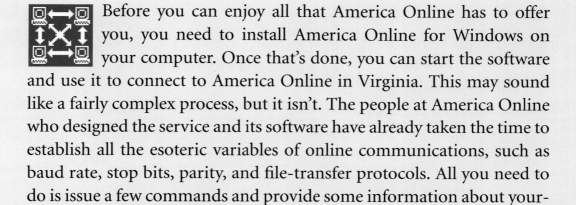Before you can enjoy all that America Online has to offer you, you need to install America Online for Windows on your computer. Once that's done, you can start the software and use it to connect to America Online in Virginia. This may sound like a fairly complex process, but it isn't. The people at America Online who designed the service and its software have already taken the time to establish all the esoteric variables of online communications, such as baud rate, stop bits, parity, and file-transfer protocols. All you need to do is issue a few commands and provide some information about yourself. The software and the service do the rest.

**Important:** Before proceeding any further, be sure that your computer is equipped with a modem, that the modem is in good working order, and that the modem is properly connected to your computer and to an active telephone outlet. If you are unfamiliar with modems, you might want to ask a computer-savvy friend or family member to check out your modem setup for you. *America Online for Windows will not work properly if your modem is not set up properly.*

# How to Install America Online for Windows

After turning on your computer and starting Windows, the basic installation procedure is simple: You place an installation disk in your floppy-disk drive, issue a command, and answer a few basic questions. Then your computer copies the appropriate information from the installation disk to your computer's hard disk. Depending on the speed of your computer, the entire process should take only a minute or two.

**TIP SHEET**

▶ **Some computers are sold with America Online for Windows already installed. If your computer's Program Manager already contains an America Online program group and program item, skip ahead to the next page.**

▶ **If you don't have any installation disks at all, there are several ways to get some. The quickest but most expensive method is to go to a computer store and buy one. A slightly slower but much less expensive alternative is to call America Online at 1-800-827-6364 and ask them to send you a free disk (or disks).**

▶ **Although the America Online installation program is designed to work flawlessly, problems do sometimes occur. If you experience a problem during installation, don't panic—the worst that will happen is that you'll have to start over. If you get completely stuck, call America Online for help at 1-800-827-6364.**

▶ **As soon as the installation is finished, you can start America Online for Windows and connect to America Online. Turn the page to see how.**

Make sure the disk fits the floppy-disk drive.

▶ **1** Your copy of America Online for Windows is on one or more 3½-inch or 5¼-inch floppy disks. To hold these disks during installation, your computer may have one 3½-inch floppy-disk drive, one 5¼-inch floppy-disk drive, two drives of the same size, or—the most convenient arrangement—one drive of each size. If your installation disks don't fit any of your floppy-disk drives, call America Online at 1-800-827-6364 for a free replacement.

**8** Finally, a dialog box opens to tell you that the installation is complete. Click on OK to close the dialog box and return to Program Manager. There, you'll see a new program group window, entitled America Online, containing the America Online program item.

**7** Sit back as the installation program copies information from the installation disk to your hard drive. If you are installing from multiple disks, you'll be asked to insert the other disk(s) when appropriate.

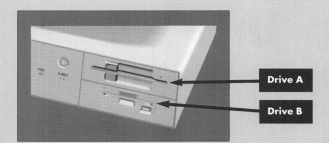

**2** You need to know the *drive letter* of the floppy-disk drive you'll be using to install America Online for Windows. If your computer has only one floppy-disk drive, then it is drive A. If your computer has two floppy-disk drives, then the top or left drive is probably drive A, and the bottom or right drive is probably drive B.

**3** If you have only one installation disk, insert it in the appropriately sized floppy-disk drive. If you have multiple installation disks, insert the disk labeled Disk 1. **Important:** To be sure you're installing a version of America Online for Windows that will work well with this book, check your installation disk(s) for the number *1.1* or *1.5* and the phrase *for Windows*.

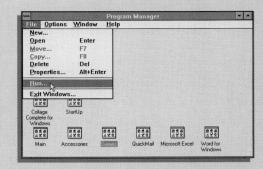

**4** In Program Manager, choose Run from the File menu. (Click on File in the menu bar, and then click on Run in the File menu.)

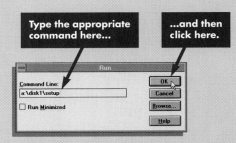

**6** After a few moments, the America Online installation program starts, and opens a dialog box to welcome you. Click on Install. If you're installing version 1.1, click on Continue instead, and then click on Continue again in the next dialog box.

**5** Next, a dialog box entitled Run opens. In the Command Line text box, type **a:\disk1\setup** if the installation disk is in drive A, or **b:\disk1\setup** if the disk is in drive B. If you're installing version 1.1, instead type **a:\install** or **b:\install**. Then click on the OK button (or press the Enter key).

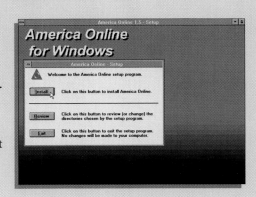

# How to Sign On to America Online for the First Time

When you start America Online (AOL) for Windows for the first time, the software automatically guides you through the process of *signing on* (connecting) to AOL. This process is fairly automated; however, you should make some preparations ahead of time. First, locate the registration number and password that came with your installation disks. Second, decide how you're going to pay for your AOL membership (VISA, checking account, and so on), and have that information ready. Finally, pick out several *screen names* for yourself. A screen name is a unique nickname of 3 to 10 characters (including spaces) that you use to identify yourself to AOL; having several names ready is helpful in case your first choice is not available.

**TIP SHEET**

▶ Because AOL is constantly changing, your computer screen may differ from the ones shown here. Just read each message carefully, and everything will probably work just fine.

▶ When choosing a password (step 6), be sure to specify one that you'll remember, but that no one else is likely to guess. Of course, your password's no good if *you* don't remember it, so write it down and put it in a safe place.

▶ Traditionally, AOL gives every new member 10 hours of free connect time (starting the moment you see the Welcome! window in step 7) and one month of free membership. As you sign on for the first time, though, be sure to read each message carefully to see what you're getting for free, and how much things are going to cost after that.

▶ To learn how to disconnect from AOL, turn the page.

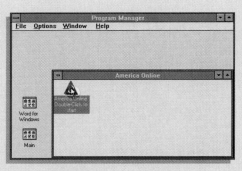

▶ **1** If necessary, open the America Online program group. Then double-click on the America Online program item. (See Chapter 2 if you need help with these operations.)

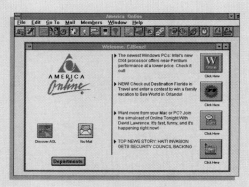

**7** After working your way through that long parade of dialog boxes and windows, you'll finally see a Welcome! window similar to this one. You are now successfully signed on to the AOL service for the first time!

**6** Continue to read and carefully follow the on-screen directions. You'll first be asked to provide some personal information (name, address, and so on). Then you'll be given some information on the cost of AOL membership, asked to select a billing method (VISA, MasterCard, American Express, Discover, or your checking account) and enter the necessary information about that method; you'll be asked to choose a screen name; then asked to choose a password (to prevent other people from using your AOL account); and then you'll see some pointers on exploring AOL.

**2** A dialog box opens asking you to confirm some settings about your physical location, and modem and telephone setup. If these settings are correct, click on Yes, or click on OK if you're installing version 1.1. (If you're not sure about these settings, ask a knowledgeable family member or friend.) Otherwise, click on No, or on Other Options if you're installing version 1.1, to reset the options as necessary.

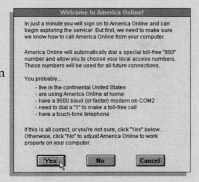

**3** Read and carefully follow the on-screen directions, clicking on OK or Continue as necessary to move on to the next dialog box or window. After a few dialog boxes,

the software will automatically dial a toll-free (1-800) number to help you determine your local AOL *access numbers*. Access numbers are local telephone numbers that AOL for Windows uses to connect to AOL; this saves you the cost of making long-distance telephone calls to Virginia.

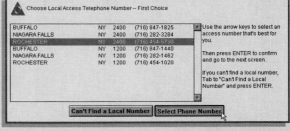

**4** Once AOL for Windows has successfully connected to the toll-free number, you will be asked to provide your local area code. Once you do, you'll be given a list of telephone numbers in or near that area code. Select a local number (one that you can call without incurring a long-distance charge), and then click on Select Phone Number.

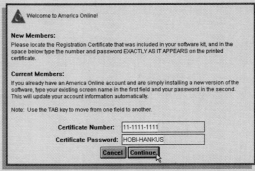

**5** You'll be asked to select a secondary local access number (as a backup in case your first number is busy) and to confirm your two choices. Then AOL for Windows will disconnect from the toll-free number and call one of your local access numbers. Once connected, you'll be asked to provide the registration number and password that came with your installation disks. Type these in carefully, and then click on Continue. Be sure to use the information included with *your* installation disk(s), *not* the information shown here.

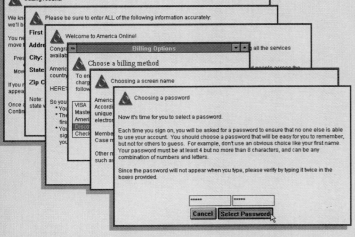

# How to Leave and Return to America Online

Once you've signed on to AOL, the clock starts ticking. Don't panic; you probably have some free time coming to you, and even after using that up, few people spend so much time on AOL that it breaks the family budget. However, prudent use of your online time will save you money in the long run. The most important step in using online time efficiently is to learn how to *sign off* (disconnect) from AOL. Even if you're just getting up to get a drink, go ahead and sign off; it's easy to do and easy to sign back on, and it saves you money. Let's see how to sign off and sign on.

▶ **1** Anytime you're on line, to sign off choose Exit from the File menu. (Or double-click on the application window's Control Menu box.) A dialog box opens to ask if you really want to sign off.

**TIP SHEET**

▶ **If you inadvertently close the Welcome window, you can reopen it by choosing Set Up & Sign On from the Go To menu.**

▶ **If you want to save yourself the trouble of typing your password each time you sign on, you can *store* your password. To do so, choose Preferences from the Members menu, click on Passwords, type your password in the appropriate box, and then click on OK. (You can do all of this while you're signed off.) If you store your password, bear in mind that anyone who has access to your computer can then use your AOL account.**

▶ **As you explore AOL, your screen can become filled with many document windows. Although you can close or minimize these windows (see Chapter 2), don't waste your time with these actions if you're going to sign off anyway. Instead, simply sign off. When you sign back on, your document windows will have been closed for you.**

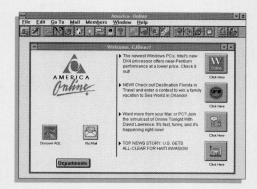

**8** If your sign-on is successful, you'll be welcomed back to AOL.

**2** If you want to sign off from AOL but keep the AOL for Windows software running, click on Yes. Then skip to step 4. (You'll learn in later chapters some advantages of leaving the software running even after you've signed off.)

**3** If you want to sign off from AOL *and* exit AOL for Windows, click on Exit Application. Then skip to step 5.

**4** If you clicked on Yes, your computer will disconnect from AOL, and the Goodbye From America Online! window will open.

**5** If you clicked on Exit Application, AOL for Windows will close, and you'll be returned to the Program Manager. To restart the software, double-click on the America Online program item; a Welcome window will open.

Type your password here...

...and then click here.

**7** AOL for Windows dials one of your local access numbers, makes the connection to America Online, and checks your password.

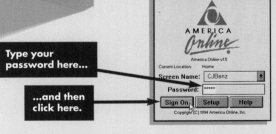

**6** Whether you see the Goodbye From America Online! or the Welcome window, you sign back on the same way: Type your password in the Password text box (for security reasons, your password will display as asterisks), and then click on Sign On. (To instead close AOL for Windows, choose Exit from the File menu. Version 1.1 users must then click on Yes.)

## CHAPTER 4

# Exploring America Online

 AOL has so much to offer that it is divided into eight separate *departments*, from News & Finance to Games & Entertainment. Each department in turn is subdivided into *areas* (also known as *services* or *features*). Even with all this organization, however, it's easy to become overwhelmed by the immense amount of available information.

Relax. Along with its neatly categorized information, AOL and AOL for Windows together provide many tools to help you get around, including the Toolbar, a Directory of Services, and keywords. This chapter shows you how to use these tools. In addition, you'll learn how to keep track of your online time and charges, so that you don't inadvertently break the family budget in your enthusiasm to explore.

So put on your pith helmet and some khaki shorts, fill your canteen, and hold on tight to your mouse and keyboard—you're going exploring!

**Note:** AOL is immense, and it gets bigger every day as new information and new services are added. Because of the size and constant growth of this online service, no book can possibly cover its every aspect. What this book does, instead, is show you many of AOL's most useful and interesting features, while teaching you about tools that you can use to efficiently explore AOL on your own. So come with us as we explore, but if you get the urge to strike out on your own, go ahead—we promise to wait for you.

# How to Use the Toolbar

The Toolbar (known as the Flashbar in version 1.1) sits right below the menu bar. It contains icons to help you get around in AOL, as well as to help you send information to and save information from AOL. Many Toolbar icons are shortcuts for commands you would otherwise issue from menus. To use a Toolbar icon, simply click on it. We'll show you many of these icons in use throughout this book.

**TIP SHEET**

▶ Although four Toolbar icons (Compose Mail, Download Manager, Print, and Save) can often be used off line, the rest are available only for online use. When Toolbar icons are unavailable, they usually appear dimmed.

▶ You *must* use the mouse (or some other pointing device) to access the Toolbar. If you're working without a pointing device, you'll need to use the menu bar instead. For the Toolbar icon with no direct menu equivalent (File Search), you can use keywords instead, as described later in this chapter.

▶ Similar to Toolbar icons, the buttons you see in the Welcome! window when you first sign on can also help you get around AOL. Many of these buttons change regularly, so we can't really describe them here with any precision. However, feel free to use them to explore on your own.

▶ **1** Click on the Read New Mail icon to see a list of any electronic mail that you've received. This is a shortcut for choosing Read New Mail from the Mail menu. To open a form for sending electronic mail to others, click on the Compose Mail icon. This is a shortcut for choosing Compose Mail from the Mail menu. (Chapter 7 shows you how to send and receive electronic mail.)

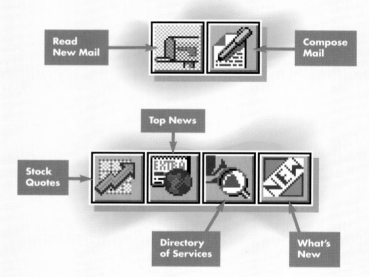

**9** Click on the Print icon to open the Print or Print Text dialog box, from which you can send the contents of the current document window to your printer. This is a shortcut for choosing Print from the File menu. Click on the Save icon to open the Save As or Save Text As dialog box, from which you can send the contents of the current document window to a hard- or floppy-disk file. This is a shortcut for choosing Save from the File menu. The Print and Save icons work only when the current document window contains information suitable for printing or saving.

**2** Click on any one of the eight department icons to go to AOL's departments: News & Finance, People Connection, Lifestyles & Interests, Games & Entertainment, Learning & Reference, Travel & Shopping, Computing & Software, or Members' Online Support. These icons are all shortcuts for choosing Departments from the Go To menu. (You'll learn more about AOL's departments throughout this book.)

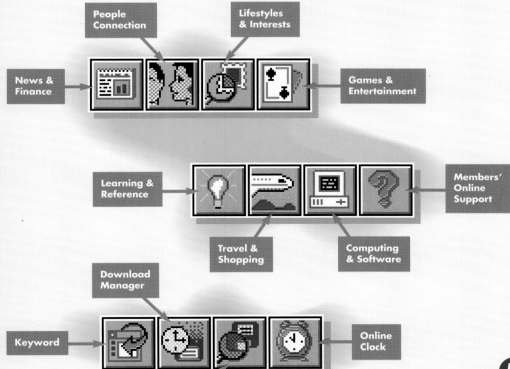

People Connection

Lifestyles & Interests

News & Finance

Games & Entertainment

Learning & Reference

Members' Online Support

Travel & Shopping

Computing & Software

Download Manager

Keyword

Online Clock

File Search

Print

Save

**3** Click on the Stock Quotes icon to go to the Quotes & Portfolios area, and click on the Top News icon to go to the Top News area. These icons are shortcuts for choosing the same areas in the Go To menu. (Chapter 5 shows you how to use these two areas.)

**4** Click on the Directory of Services icon as a shortcut for choosing Directory of Services from the Go To menu. (You'll learn how to use the Directory on the next page.)

**5** Click on the What's New icon to go to the New Features & Services area. This is a shortcut for choosing New Services from the Go To menu. (As you might expect, this area describes AOL's newest features and services.)

**6** Click on the Keyword icon to open the Go To Keyword window. This is a shortcut for choosing Keyword from the Go To menu. (You'll learn about keywords later in this chapter.)

**8** Click on the Online Clock icon to see the current time and how long you've been on line during your current AOL session. In version 1.5, this is a shortcut for choosing Online Clock from the Go To menu. (You'll learn more about the online clock later in this chapter.)

**7** Click on the Download Manager icon as a shortcut for choosing Download Manager from the File menu. Click on the File Search icon to open the File Search window. This item is not available on any menu. (Chapter 16 shows you how to search for and download files.)

# How to Use the Directory of Services

One of the challenges of using an online service as large and diverse as AOL is finding out what's available. It's like exploring a large, unfamiliar city without a printed tour guide: You can wander around for hours or even days before stumbling upon something that really intrigues you. That's where AOL's *Directory of Services* comes in. Like a well-designed tour guide, the Directory provides a wealth of descriptions that help you quickly and easily identify AOL areas that might interest you. As an added bonus, the Directory can even transport you to any described area.

**TIP SHEET**

▶ **An active More button (see step 5) is a common sight near AOL list boxes; it indicates that the current list is only a partial list. (Note the line above the list box in step 5—"Items 1–20 of 28 matching entries"—indicating that eight more list items are available.) Whenever you display a list that exceeds 20 items, AOL generally shows you only the first 20 items, and then activates the More button. Click on that button to add more items to the list—up to 20 at a time. Once every available item is listed, the More button will dim.**

▶ **An area description often lists the area's *location* (see the bottom of the list box in step 6). The location shows how to reach the described area without using a shortcut such as the Directory of Services.**

▶ **The Directory of Services is just one example of AOL's many *searchable databases*. You'll learn more about them in Chapter 9.**

▶ **❶** Make sure you're signed on to AOL, and then click on the Toolbar's Directory of Services icon. (Or choose Directory of Services from the Go To menu.)

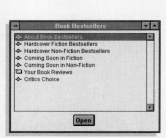

**❽** You are directly transported to that service.

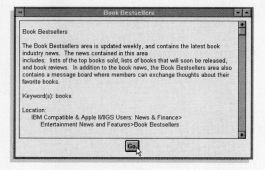

**❼** To explore the described service further, click on Go.

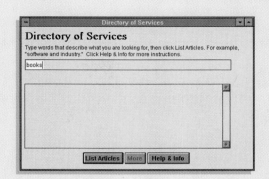

**2** A Directory of Services window opens. Double-click on Search the Directory of Services.

**3** A second Directory of Services window opens. In the blank text box at the top of this window, type a *search criterion*. A search criterion is a word or words that indicate the type of service you are seeking. For example, if you want to play a game, you could type **games**; if you're interested in book reviews, you could type **books**.

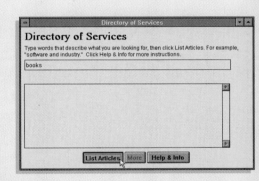

**4** Click on List Articles.

**6** A new window opens, containing a description of the service you selected. Use the scroll bar as necessary to read the service's description.

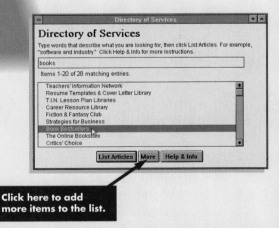

Click here to add more items to the list.

**5** The window's list box now displays the services related to your search criterion. If you don't see a service that interests you, scroll down through the list. If there are more services available than will fit in the list box, the More button will be available for you to click to list additional services. Once you find a listing that *does* interest you, double-click on it.

# How to Use Keywords

**O**nce you start getting familiar with AOL and discovering certain departments and areas that you want to visit regularly, you'll come to appreciate keywords. Using a keyword is like taking a taxi: You give the driver an address, and then sit back for the ride. You don't have to know the route because the driver takes care of that for you. New in town and don't know any addresses? No problem—just like a friendly and knowledgeable taxi driver, AOL will provide some address suggestions for you.

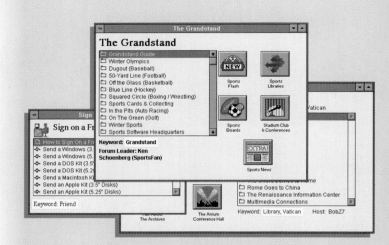

**▶ ❶** When you visit an area that you want to come back to, look for the area's keyword. Keywords are usually displayed near the bottom of the area's window. Make a mental note of the keyword, or jot it down. (If you haven't explored enough yet to find a suitable keyword, don't worry; we'll help you out on that in a moment.)

### TIP SHEET

▶ **You will find keywords mentioned all over AOL, inviting you to jump from one place to another. If you're intrigued, give in to the urge. When it's time to return to your original window, simply close or minimize any new windows you've opened. Or, try returning to a previous window by choosing its name from the Window menu.**

▶ **AOL's keyword lists contain only some of the many keywords available, and not every area displays a keyword, even if one exists. So once you find a keyword that works for you, hold on to it; good keywords are like gold.**

▶ **If you find that you use certain keywords frequently, or if you just have trouble remembering your favorite keywords, try adding them to the Go To menu. To do this, choose Edit Go To Menu from the Go To menu.**

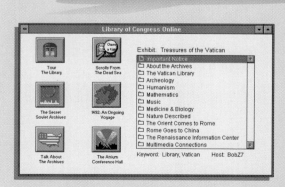

**❽** You are directly transported to the department or area specified by your keyword.

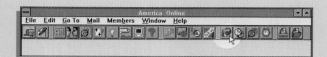

**2** Let's see how to use a keyword. Make sure you're signed on to AOL, and then click on the Toolbar's Keyword icon. (Or choose Keyword from the Go To menu.)

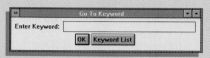

**3** The Go To Keyword window opens. If you know which keyword you want to use, skip now to step 7. Otherwise, continue on to step 4.

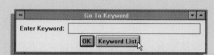

**4** If you don't know which keyword you want to use, click on Keyword List.

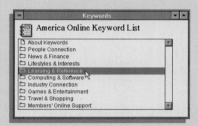

**5** The Keywords window opens, listing AOL's departments. Double-click on the name of the department that most likely houses the area you want to visit.

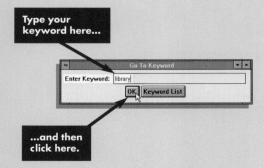

Type your keyword here...

...and then click here.

**7** Type your keyword in the Enter Keyword text box, and then click on OK. Note that keywords are not *case sensitive*; that is, it doesn't matter if you type a keyword in all uppercase (*LIBRARY*), lowercase (*library*), or some mixture of the two (*LiBrArY*). You'll still end up in the same place.

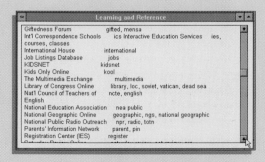

**6** A new window opens, listing keywords associated with that department and its areas. Scroll through the list as necessary to find the appropriate keyword. Make a note of it, and then click once again on the Toolbar's Keyword icon (see step 2).

# How to Keep Track of Your Online Time and Charges

After using up any free or credited minutes you might have, every extra minute you spend on AOL costs money. It's not a tremendous amount of money, but it's still a good idea to keep track of your online time and charges so that things don't get out of hand. An unexpectedly large online service bill is bad for you (because you have to pay it), as well as for AOL (because then they have an unhappy customer). To help prevent such a problem, AOL makes it easy for you to see how long you've been on line during your current session. Or if you want to see your overall charges for the current billing cycle, AOL can show you that, too.

**TIP SHEET**

▶ **Billing terms**—such as how many minutes you're credited when you first join AOL, your monthly membership fee, how many free minutes are included in that fee, and so on—might differ among members and across time. To see the exact billing terms of *your* membership, repeat steps 3 and 4, click on Explain Billing Terms, and then click on Open.

▶ Your current month's billing summary reflects all of your chargeable online time, *except* for the current online session. For the most accurate summary, sign off and back on again, and then look at the summary immediately.

▶ *Free minutes* are the minutes you get every month as part of your monthly membership fee. *Credited minutes* are additional minutes that you might receive, for example, as a gift for joining AOL or as compensation for some online difficulty you've had.

▶ **1** To see how long you've been on line during your current session, click on the Toolbar's Online Clock icon. (Or in version 1.5, choose Online Clock from the Go To menu.)

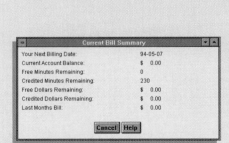

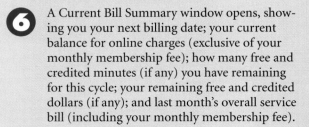

**6** A Current Bill Summary window opens, showing you your next billing date; your current balance for online charges (exclusive of your monthly membership fee); how many free and credited minutes (if any) you have remaining for this cycle; your remaining free and credited dollars (if any); and last month's overall service bill (including your monthly membership fee).

**2** A dialog box opens, show-ing you the current time and how long you've been on line. Click on OK to close the dialog box.

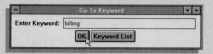

**3** To see all of your charges for the current monthly billing cycle, use the keyword **billing**.

**4** A dialog box opens, indicating that you are about to enter a free area. (Free areas are discussed in Chapter 10.) Click on Yes.

**5** A Billing Information and Changes window opens, listing a variety of options. Click on Current Month's Billing Summary, and then click on Open. (Or simply double-click on Current Month's Billing Summary.)

## CHAPTER 5

# Keeping Up with the News

You're probably used to getting most of your news from the newspaper, magazines, television, and radio. These are all good news sources, but each has its drawbacks. Newspapers and magazines generally provide good, in-depth news coverage, but by their very nature they contain news that may be anywhere from many hours to many months old. Both television and radio can provide up-to-the-minute news, but these stories tend to be short because of limited air time, and unless you regularly tape the news, you need to watch or listen at specific times.

Also, the amount of advertising carried by most newspapers, magazines, and television and radio stations can be overwhelming. In fact, sometimes there are more ads than news.

Enter AOL. Its news is substantial and up-to-date, available 24 hours a day, and ad-free. Plus, it's easy and fun to use. This chapter covers some of AOL's many news offerings, including the top news articles, weather forecasts, stock quotes, and magazines.

So the next time you want to catch up on the news, leave that newspaper on the porch, put down the remote control, and instead reach for your keyboard and mouse. Your newest (and perhaps soon-to-be favorite) news source is only a few keystrokes and mouse clicks away.

# How to Read Today's Top News

S o you're interested in reading today's top news articles. Are you interested in news in general, or perhaps something more specific, such as the top business, sports, or entertainment news? Or, perhaps your time is limited and you just want a brief news summary. No problem; AOL is ready for you on all counts. Whenever you're on line, the top news is only a click away.

**TIP SHEET**

▶ **The Welcome! window that opens when you first sign on to AOL may contain a button for accessing top news stories. If you prefer, you probably can use this button instead of doing step 1.**

▶ **To print or save a news summary or article for offline use, open the article's window, and then click on the Toolbar's Print or Save icon. These two icons work not only for saving and printing news articles, but for just about any AOL window that contains a lot of text.**

▶ **To access a searchable database of news articles, click on the Top News window's Search News button. To learn more about using searchable databases, see Chapter 9.**

▶ **Top News is only one small part of AOL's regular news offerings. To see more news options, click on the Toolbar's News & Finance icon or use the keyword *news*.**

▶ **①** Make sure you're signed on to AOL, and then click on the Toolbar's Top News icon. (Or choose Top News from the Go To menu.)

**⑧** To read another article, close the current article window, and repeat steps 5 through 7.

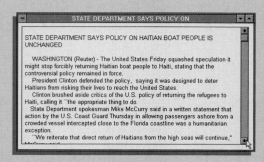

**⑦** The selected article displays in its own window. Scroll as necessary to read it.

**2** The Top News window opens, listing the headlines of today's top general news articles.

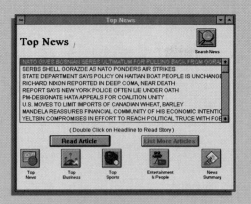

**3** To start out with a brief news summary, click on News Summary. Otherwise, skip to step 5.

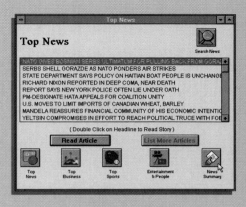

**4** An Hourly News Summary window opens, providing brief versions of the hour's top news articles. Once you've finished reading the news summary, close the window. (Double-click on the window's Control Menu box.)

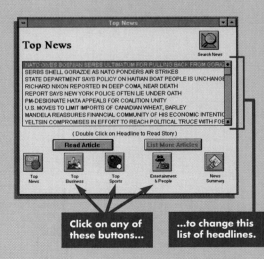

**Click on any of these buttons...** **...to change this list of headlines.**

**6** Scroll through the list box as necessary to find an article that interests you. Once you do, click on that article's headline, and then click on Read Article. (Or simply double-click on the article's headline.)

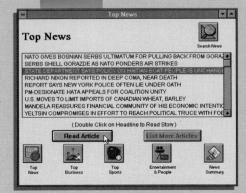

**5** If you're interested in reading more detailed news articles, skip to step 6. If you want to read specifically business, sports, or entertainment news, then click on either Top Business, Top Sports, or Entertainment & People. This will change the list of headlines accordingly.

# How to Check a Weather Forecast

Is it going to rain tomorrow? What kind of weather can you expect on your upcoming weekend trip? Weather can be very critical news to you at times, but unless the weather is especially severe or unusual, general weather forecasts rarely make it into AOL's Top News area. To see general weather forecasts, you must instead visit AOL's (what else?) Weather area. There you'll find five-day weather forecasts for just about every major city in the world, and these forecasts are available 24 hours a day. So the next time you're wondering whether you should walk out of the house in a slicker or a swimsuit, ask AOL.

▶ **1** Make sure you're signed on to AOL, and then use the keyword **weather**. (Or click on the Toolbar's News & Finance icon, and then double-click on Weather.)

### TIP SHEET

▶ **To make weather forecasts easier to read, try maximizing the forecast window as we have done in steps 5 and 8. (Chapter 2 shows you how to maximize windows.)**

▶ **As you can see in step 2, AOL's weather area offers more than just general weather forecasts. You can also check ski reports, weather-related news, and weather maps in color. You can even *discuss* the weather with other AOL members. This is typical of AOL: A little something for everyone.**

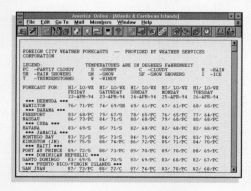

**8** A weather forecast window opens, listing five-day forecasts for your selected area's major cities. Scroll as necessary to see the desired forecast.

**2** The Weather window opens, listing various options for retrieving weather information. To check a weather forecast for a U.S. city, click on U.S. Cities Forecasts, and then click on Open. (Or double-click on U.S. Cities Forecasts.) To check a forecast for a foreign city, skip to step 6.

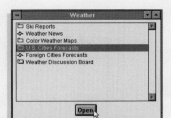

**3** The U.S. Cities Forecasts window opens. Instead of making you scroll through a list of 50 states, the list box contains just a few alphabetized state groups. Click on the group that contains the desired state, and then click on Open. (Or double-click on the state group.)

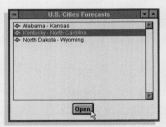

**4** Another window opens, listing just those states contained in the group you chose in step 3. Scroll as necessary, click on the desired state, and then click on Open. (Or double-click on the state.)

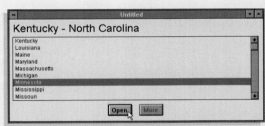

**5** A weather forecast window opens, listing five-day forecasts for your selected state's major cities. Scroll as necessary to see the desired forecast. To also see a weather forecast for a foreign city, return to the Weather window shown in step 2 (close windows as necessary, or choose Weather from the Window menu), and then continue on to step 6. Otherwise, you can skip the rest of this activity.

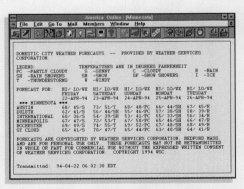

**6** To check a weather forecast for a foreign city, click on Foreign Cities Forecasts, and then click on Open. (Or double-click on Foreign Cities Forecast.)

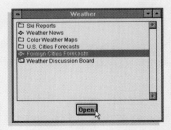

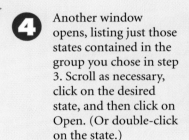

**7** Another window opens, listing various countries, continents, and regions around the world. Scroll as necessary, click on the desired country, continent, or region, and then click on Open. (Or double-click on the desired country, continent, or region.)

# How to Get Stock Quotes

**D**o you own stock? Are you interested in seeing how your stocks are doing? If so, check out AOL's *Stock Quotes*. They are updated frequently throughout each business day, and include a wealth of information—from current price to the stock's price/earnings (P/E) ratio.

▶ **1** Make sure you're signed on to AOL, and then click on the Toolbar's Stock Quotes icon. (Or choose Stock Quotes from the Go To menu.)

**8** To look up another stock symbol and get another quote, return to the Search Symbols window, and repeat step 6.

**7** A Quote Detail window opens, listing your chosen stock's quote.

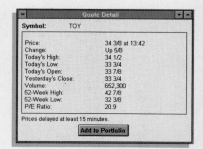

| | |
|---|---|
| Quote Detail | |
| **Symbol:** | TOY |
| Price: | 34 3/8 at 13:42 |
| Change: | Up 5/8 |
| Today's High: | 34 1/2 |
| Today's Low: | 33 3/4 |
| Today's Open: | 33 7/8 |
| Yesterday's Close: | 33 3/4 |
| Volume: | 652,300 |
| 52-Week High: | 42 7/8 |
| 52-Week Low: | 32 3/8 |
| P/E Ratio: | 20.9 |

Prices delayed at least 15 minutes.

**Add to Portfolio**

**TIP SHEET**

▶ **Once you've found a stock symbol you need, make a note of it. As you can see, knowing the symbol up front can save you quite a few steps.**

▶ **If you're new to the world of stocks and interested in learning more, check out AOL's personal finance area, Your Money. To get there, use the keyword *your money*.**

▶ **The Add To Portfolio button, shown in a number of screens on this page, enables you to set up an online portfolio of stocks just for fun (no real money involved). For more information on creating your own portfolio, click on the Help And Info button in the Quotes & Portfolios window.**

▶ **You can also buy real stocks with real money, through AOL's TradePlus feature. To access this feature, click on the TradePlus button in the Quotes & Portfolios window.**

**2** The Quotes & Portfolios window opens, providing a variety of options for retrieving stock information. Every publicly traded stock has a unique *stock symbol*—an abbreviation of the company's name. If you know it, type the symbol for your desired stock in the Enter Symbol text box, and click on Get Quote. If you don't know the symbol for your stock, skip to step 4.

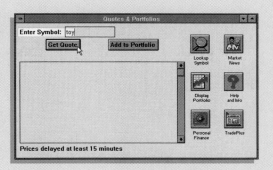

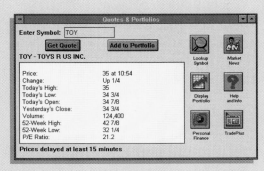

**3** If AOL recognizes your stock symbol, then the window's list box displays that stock's current quote. To get an additional quote, delete your stock symbol from the Enter Symbol text box, and repeat step 2. Otherwise, you can skip the rest of this activity.

**4** To have AOL help you determine a stock symbol, click on Lookup Symbol.

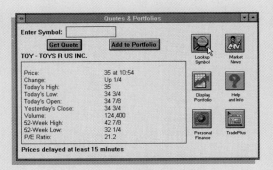

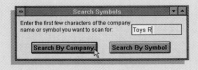

**6** The Symbols window opens, listing the companies and their stock symbols that resemble your search criterion. Scroll as necessary, click on the desired stock symbol and company name, and then click on Get Quote. (Or double-click on the stock symbol and company name.) If you can't find your desired symbol and company by scrolling, click on the More button to add more items to the list.

**5** The Search Symbols window opens, providing you two ways to search for stock symbols: by company and by symbol. If you know the company name, type the first few characters of that name into the text box, and then click on Search By Company. If you only know part of the stock symbol, type the first few characters of that symbol in the text box, and then click on Search By Symbol.

# How to Read an Online Magazine

One reason magazines are such popular information sources is that they are so specialized. Thousands of different magazines are published each month, on subjects ranging from airplanes to zymurgy. You might read only one or two articles in your daily newspaper, but your monthly juggling journal is probably ragged because you read *every* article. On AOL you can read dozens of the most popular magazines—on line. And if you don't see your favorite magazine there yet, just wait. Online magazines offer many of the same advantages as other online news sources: 24-hour availability, up-to-date information, and so on. Who knows? Maybe you'll never have to pay for a magazine subscription again!

## TIP SHEET

▶ **Once you know a particular magazine's keyword (see Chapter 4), you can use that keyword to bypass The Newsstand window and jump directly to that magazine.**

▶ **Because of their varying specialties, you can also find magazines located in various AOL departments and areas that cover particular subjects. The Newsstand area simply makes many magazines easier to find.**

▶ **Some magazines offer their own message boards and searchable databases. To learn more about using message boards, see Chapter 6. To learn more about using searchable databases, see Chapter 9.**

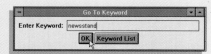

▶ **1** Make sure you're signed on to AOL, and then use the keyword **newsstand**. (Or choose Departments from the Go To menu, and then click on The Newsstand.)

**8** To read another magazine article, return to the starting magazine window, and then repeat steps 5 through 7. To switch to another magazine, return to The Newsstand window (shown in steps 2 and 3), and repeat steps 3 through 7.

**7** Scroll to read the article.

**2** The Newsstand window opens, listing many of AOL's magazines and newspapers. For easier access, some of the most popular or newly available magazines and newspapers may also appear on their own buttons.

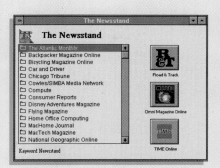

**3** Scroll as necessary, and then double-click on the desired magazine. Or, click on the magazine's button if one is available.

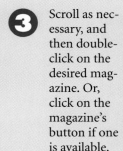

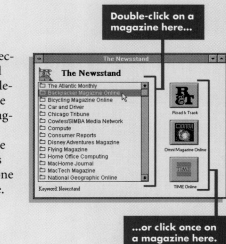

Double-click on a magazine here...

...or click once on a magazine here.

**4** Just as every printed magazine is different, so is every online magazine window. Typical online magazine windows, however, include a list box that serves as an electronic table of contents. Most windows also display buttons that enable you to do anything from learning more about the magazine to sending an electronic letter to the editor.

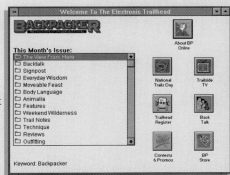

**5** To read a magazine article, your best bet is to scroll through the list box to find something that interests you, and then double-click on that item. (If you prefer to be a bit more daring, go ahead and click on one of the buttons; there's no telling where one might take you.)

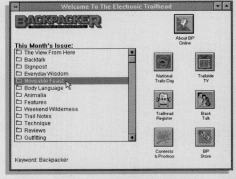

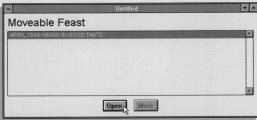

**6** Another window opens, displaying either a magazine article or another list box. If the window displays an article, you can proceed to step 7. If the window displays a list box, scroll as necessary to find an item that interests you, select that item, and then click on Open. (If an Open button isn't available, then double-click on the list item instead.) Repeat this step as necessary until an article window opens.

## CHAPTER 6

# Using Message Boards

 So far in this book, we've only introduced you to profession-
ally produced AOL features. For example, when you read a
news article or weather forecast (see Chapter 5), that information generally is provided by an AOL employee or vendor who's
compensated for doing so. That's AOL's *professional* side—but AOL
also has a rich and intriguing *personal* side.

AOL isn't just a collection of impersonal electronic information; it's
also an electronic *community* comprising AOL's many members. In this
and the next two chapters, we'll show you ways to interact with other
AOL members, through message boards, electronic mail, and chat
rooms.

This chapter introduces *message boards*—sometimes known as *bulletin boards*. Like the cork-and-pushpin message boards you see in many
grocery stores, libraries, and laundromats, AOL's electronic message
boards offer places for people to openly post messages (often called *postings*) for other people to read. In most cases, messages are exchanged
primarily among members, but some boards do specialize in exchanging messages between members and AOL employees or vendors.

Unlike those grocery-store boards, though, AOL's message boards
don't usually contain many one-way messages such as "Bake Sale This
Friday." Rather, these electronic boards promote lively, multiple-
member discussions and debates on subjects ranging from politics to
health to fine dining. In this way, AOL's electronic message boards are
more like community meetings. Read on to learn more.

# How to Peruse a Message Board

To prevent message-board chaos, AOL provides dozens of subject-specific boards. This way, members interested primarily in politics, for instance, don't have to wade through dozens of messages on health. Message boards are scattered all over AOL, so you're bound to stumble across one eventually. When you do find a board that interests you—a likely occurrence, as you'll be exploring areas that interest you, anyway—your first logical step is to peruse the board to see what kind of discussions and debates are there. This page shows you how to get to know a message board on your first visit.

▶ **If you're unsure of a board's specific purpose or how to access a unique board feature, try clicking on the Help & Info button in the board's initial window. (If this button is unavailable, see Chapter 10 for information on other sources of help.)**

▶ **To see a list of messages contained within a topic instead of jumping right to the first message, in step 5 click on the List Messages button rather than on Read 1st Message. Then, to open a listed message, click on the message and then on Read Message. (Or simply double-click on the message.)**

▶ **After you've visited a board once, or if there are too many messages for you to read in one session, try taking advantage of the Find New and Find Since buttons (available in most boards). Find New lists only messages that have been posted since your last visit to this board; Find Since lists only messages that have been posted since a date that you specify.**

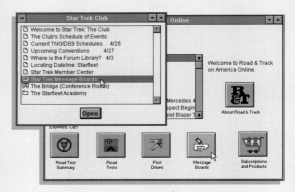

**1** As you explore AOL, keep your eye out for buttons or list-box items that lead to message boards. Generally, these buttons and items display pushpin icons and/or include the words *message* and/or *board*. To access a board using a button, click on the button; to access a message using a list-box item, double-click on the item.

**8** To read the messages in another topic, return to the topics window and repeat steps 5 through 7. To read messages in another category, return to the subjects window, and repeat steps 4 through 7.

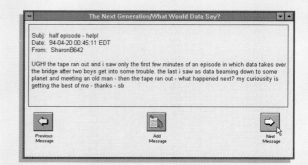

**7** When you're done reading the current message, click on Next Message to display the next message in your selected topic. (You can also review earlier messages by clicking on Previous Message.) Repeat this step as desired to read the remaining messages. Once you've read every message in the current topic, the Next Message button dims.

**2** Like online magazines (see Chapter 5), every message board is different. Typically, though, message boards use electronic *folders* (similar in function to the manila folders used in a filing cabinet) to divide and organize messages into separate topics. Popular message boards, like the one shown here, first divide messages into categories, which are in turn divided into topic folders.

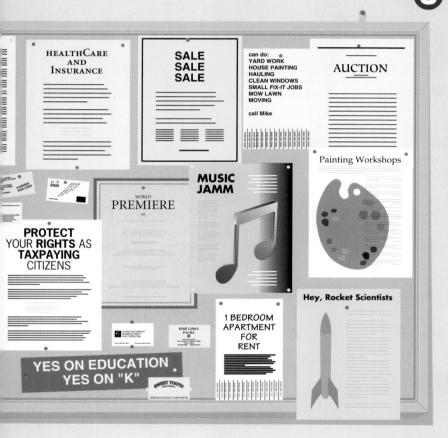

**3** The initial window for a typical message board provides a set of buttons for perusing the board. If your board is divided first into categories (like the board shown here), the window generally will display a List Categories button. If it does, click on that button and then move on to step 4. If your board is divided into topics only, there will generally be a Browse Folders button; if so, click on that button and then skip to step 5.

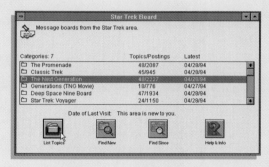

**4** A new window opens, listing available categories. Scroll to find a category that interests you, click on that category, and then click on List Topics. (Or simply double-click on the category.)

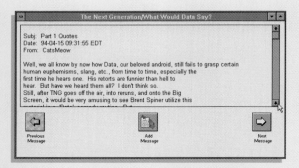

**6** The first message in the selected topic opens. Scroll to read the message.

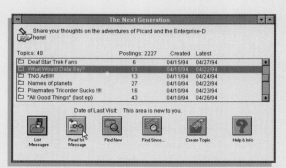

**5** A new window opens, listing available topics. Scroll to find a topic that interests you, click on that topic, and then click on Read 1st Message.

# How to Post a Message

**N**ow you know how to peruse a message board. Just perusing the board, however, is akin to listening in on a conversation but never speaking your mind. To take an *active* part in the conversation, you need to post your own messages. As with face-to-face conversations, your online messages can express opinions and insights, ask questions, give responses, or whatever—just as long as the messages are fairly meaningful and related to the topic at hand. Posting messages on a regular basis keeps your favorite message board lively and interesting for all participants and makes you an active "citizen" of the AOL community. After all, what good is a message board with no messages?

### TIP SHEET

▶ **You have virtually unlimited space when typing a message. Keep in mind, however, that very few readers have the interest or inclination to read l-o-n-n-n-g messages.**

▶ **Remember that your message may be read by hundreds or even thousands of people from varying backgrounds, so be careful what you write and how you write it. In general, avoid profanity, snide and discriminatory remarks, and personal attacks. Watch out for subtle jokes, too—without the help of body language usually present in face-to-face conversations, your message may appear to be offensive, even if you didn't intend it to be.**

▶ **If you can't find an appropriate existing topic for your message, try creating a new topic folder and posting your message there. To create a topic folder, list the topics most closely related to your new topic, and then click on Create Topic.**

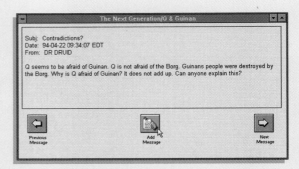

▶ **1** To respond to a specific message, open the message and then click on Add Message. For a more general message—one that isn't in direct response to another message—you can instead list the messages within an appropriate topic, and then click on Post Message. (To see how to list topic messages, see the second Tip on the previous page.)

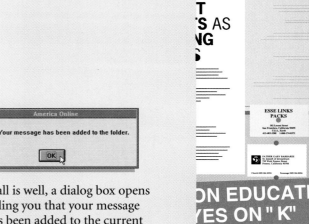

**7** If all is well, a dialog box opens telling you that your message has been added to the current topic folder. Click on OK to close the dialog box.

**6** When your message is ready to go, click on Post.

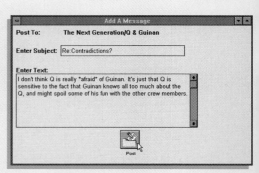

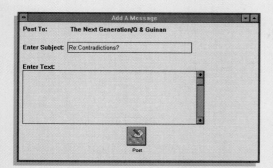

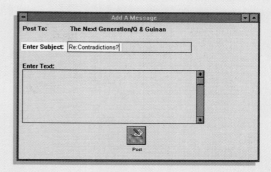

**2** Whichever button you click on, the Add A Message window opens. This is where you identify your message subject and write the body of your message.

**3** If you clicked on Add Message in step 1, then the Enter Subject text box already reflects the subject of the message to which you're responding. In general, you can leave this text as is; that makes it easier for other readers to follow the various conversations within a topic. If you instead clicked on Post Message in step 1, the Enter Subject text box will be empty; in that case, type some appropriate text here.

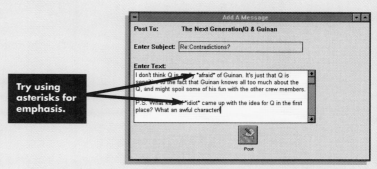

Try using asterisks for emphasis.

**4** Click in the Enter Text text box, and type your message. Avoid using all uppercase characters; IT'S LIKE SHOUTING! To add emphasis to a particular word or phrase without using uppercase, enclose that word or phrase within some *attention-getting* punctuation, such as the asterisks shown here.

**5** Once you've finished typing, use your arrow keys, Delete, and Backspace as necessary to review and edit your message thoroughly. Remember, once you post your message, there's no taking it back; this is your last chance to make sure that you're saying exactly what you mean to say.

**CHAPTER 7**

# Sending and Receiving Electronic Mail

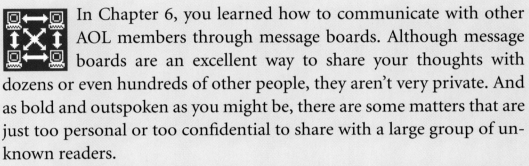 In Chapter 6, you learned how to communicate with other AOL members through message boards. Although message boards are an excellent way to share your thoughts with dozens or even hundreds of other people, they aren't very private. And as bold and outspoken as you might be, there are some matters that are just too personal or too confidential to share with a large group of unknown readers.

When you want to send private messages, try AOL's Mail feature. Like its paper counterpart, electronic mail (also known as *e-mail*) is designed for more private communications—but without the waste of paper, envelopes, and stamps. Besides the privacy factor, AOL's e-mail system has many other advantages over message boards: For instance, you don't have to depend on your recipients checking the appropriate board, because the moment they sign on, they are automatically notified of any new e-mail they've received. You can send AOL messages to many other e-mail systems (the Internet, CompuServe, MCI Mail, and so on), too. And if your recipient isn't connected to *any* e-mail system, you can use AOL's Mail to send a fax or even an old-fashioned stamp-and-envelope letter. All of these benefits, along with its ease of use, makes Mail one of AOL's most popular features.

And the U.S. Postal Service thinks self-adhesive stamps are *progress*?

# How to Send Mail to Other AOL Members

Composing and sending e-mail to other AOL members is easy. You type up a message just as you would to send it by traditional mail, but instead of going through the bother of printing the message, addressing and stamping an envelope, and running down to the corner mailbox, you just click on a few on-screen buttons. AOL e-mail is inexpensive, too. Unlike some other online services, AOL lets you send as many mail messages as you want at no extra charge. As an added bonus, you can even save yourself some online charges by composing your mail messages off line; when you're ready, you only have to sign on for the few seconds it takes to send your mail.

## TIP SHEET

▶ **If you're unsure of a recipient's screen name, try finding it in AOL's Member Directory. Sign on, and then choose Search Member Directory from the Members menu. (This directory is a searchable database; Chapter 9 describes searchable databases.) If all else fails, call your friend by (gasp!) telephone and ask for the name.**

▶ **To send multiple mail messages, perform steps 1 through 5 for each message, sign on, and then perform steps 7 and 8 for each message.**

▶ **To address the same message to more than one member, type all the screen names in the To list box, separating them with commas. Use this same technique in the CC list box to send multiple courtesy copies.**

▶ **To review, check on the status of, or even *unsend* (retrieve) mail messages that your recipients haven't yet read, sign on, and then choose Check Mail You've Sent from the Mail menu.**

**1** Start AOL for Windows, but don't sign on to AOL yet. If you're already signed on, sign off without leaving AOL for Windows. (Refer back to Chapter 3 for details.) Then click on the Toolbar's Compose Mail icon. (Or choose Compose Mail from the Mail menu.)

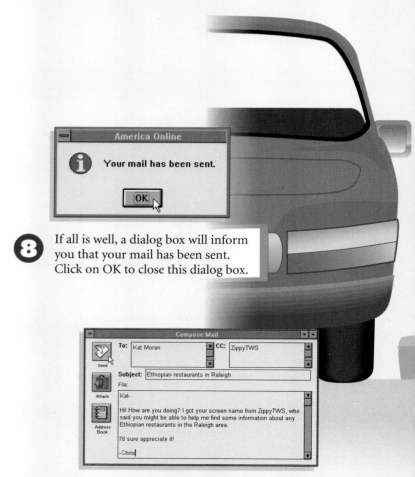

**8** If all is well, a dialog box will inform you that your mail has been sent. Click on OK to close this dialog box.

**7** In the Compose Mail window, click on Send.

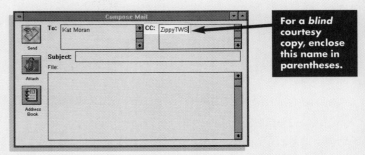

**2** A Compose Mail window opens. In the To list box, type your addressee's screen name.

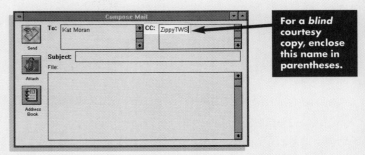

For a *blind* courtesy copy, enclose this name in parentheses.

**3** If you want to send a courtesy copy of your message to a second AOL member, type that member's screen name in the CC list box. (To send a *blind* courtesy copy—one that your addressee cannot tell you sent—enclose the screen name in parentheses.)

After signing on, move this window out of the way.

**AOL Mail**

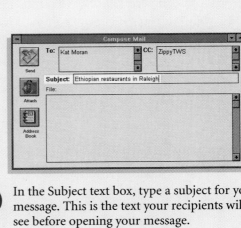

**4** In the Subject text box, type a subject for your message. This is the text your recipients will see before opening your message.

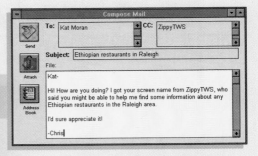

**5** In the large box at the bottom of the window, type your message. As with message-board messages, you have virtually unlimited typing space, but try to be as concise as possible. Use your arrow keys, Backspace, and Delete as necessary to review and edit your message.

**6** Move the Welcome or Goodbye from America Online! window so that it's in front of the Compose Mail window. (Either choose the window name from the Window menu, or select Set Up & Sign On in the Go To menu.) Sign on to AOL, and then minimize the online Welcome! window to get it out of the way.

# How to Read Mail You've Received

**O**ne of the nicest things about *sending* mail is that it greatly increases your chances of *receiving* mail in return. If you've been an AOL member for more than a day or so, you may already have received a mail message from AOL President Steve Case, welcoming you to the service. If you've successfully read this message, then you already know the basics of receiving mail; read this page to learn a little more. If, on the other hand, your mail has been piling up because you weren't quite sure how to look at it, then these pages will help you out.

▶ **1** You can read new mail, and you can review mail you've already read. To read new mail, continue on to step 2. To review old mail, skip to step 7.

**8** The Old Mail window opens, listing all the mail messages you've recently read. (Already-read messages are usually deleted seven days after they were originally sent.) Click on the message you want to review, and then click on Read. The message will open in its own window, as shown in step 5.

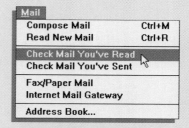

**7** To review old mail, make sure you're signed on to AOL, and then choose Check Mail You've Read from the Mail menu.

**2** Whenever you're on line, look at the Toolbar's Read New Mail icon. If the red flag is up, you've got new mail waiting for you. If the red flag is down, then you have no new mail; you'll either have to wait for someone to send you some mail, or send some mail to yourself just for testing purposes.

**3** If the red flag *is* up, click on the Read New Mail icon. (Or choose Read New Mail from the Mail menu.)

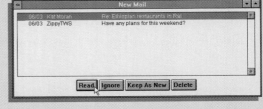

**4** A New Mail window opens, listing all the mail messages you've received but haven't yet read. Click on Read.

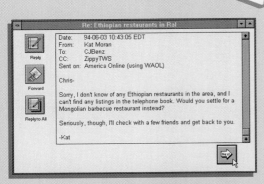

**6** If you have more than one mail message waiting, a Next button will appear in the bottom of the message window. Click on this button to display the next message, and then repeat this step as necessary to read all of your mail. Then, you can skip the rest of this activity, or continue on to review old mail.

**5** The first mail message opens in its own window. Scroll as necessary to read the message. (To keep a permanent copy of the message, you can also save or print it.)

# How to Attach a File to Mail

You probably use programs other than AOL for Windows, such as a word processor (Word, WordPerfect, Ami Pro) or a spreadsheet program (Excel, 1-2-3, Quattro Pro). So you may already know that those programs use disk files to store information in fairly complex formats. AOL's mail messages, however, are only capable of handling a very simple format: plain text. Rather than trying to translate a complex disk file into plain text—thus losing its special formatting and formulas—you can instead *attach* the file to a mail message. When you send your message, the file is copied as is to AOL's computers. When your addressee receives that message, it's a fairly simple task to then copy the file from AOL to his or her own computer.

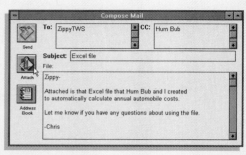

▶ **1** Start composing a mail message as you normally would. (For details, refer back to "How to Send Mail to Another AOL Member" earlier in this chapter.) In the message, explain the purpose of the file that you'll be attaching. Then click on Attach.

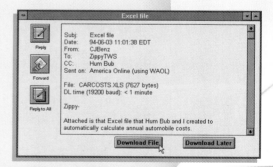
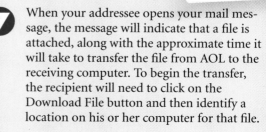

**7** When your addressee opens your mail message, the message will indicate that a file is attached, along with the approximate time it will take to transfer the file from AOL to the receiving computer. To begin the transfer, the recipient will need to click on the Download File button and then identify a location on his or her computer for that file.

**TIP SHEET**

▶ You have probably heard the terms *uploading* and *downloading*. These words describe the two directions of file transfers. Uploading is the process of transferring files from your computer to another computer. Downloading is the process of transferring files from another computer to your computer. For more information on downloading files from AOL, see Chapter 15.

▶ Although you can use one mail message to send the same file to multiple addressees, you can only attach one file to any one message.

▶ Before sending a file, make sure your addressee has the software necessary to use that file.

▶ It's illegal to send anyone copyrighted files, such as program files, without the express permission to do so.

**2** An Attach File dialog box opens. Use the Drives and Directories boxes as necessary to identify where the file is stored on your computer. Click on the file in the File Name list box, and then click on OK. (If you need help with drives and directories, consult your Windows documentation.)

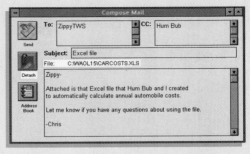

**3** When the Attach File dialog box closes, notice that two things have changed in the Compose Mail window: The location and name of your attached file now appears next to the "File:" field above the window's central list box, and the Attach button becomes a Detach button. (As you might expect, the Detach button enables you to remove the current file attachment.)

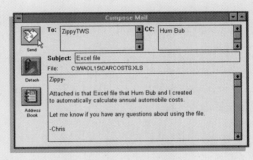

**4** If you're already on line, click on Send. If not, sign on to AOL, minimize the Welcome! window, and then click on Send.

This bar displays your progress.

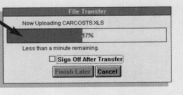

**6** Once the file transfer is complete, another File Transfer dialog box will open to inform you of that fact. Click on the OK button to close this dialog box.

**5** A File Transfer dialog box opens to display the progress of the file transfer from your computer to AOL. The length of this transfer will depend primarily on the file's size and your modem's *baud rate.* (Check your modem's documentation for information on your modem's baud rate.)

# How to Send Mail Outside of AOL

As you learned at the opening of this chapter, AOL mail isn't limited to mail among AOL members; you also have three options for sending mail to destinations *outside* of AOL. You can send messages to other e-mail systems as *Internet mail*, you can send messages to most U.S. or Canadian fax machines as *fax mail*, and you can even have messages sent via the U.S. Postal Service to any U.S. or Canadian postal address as *paper mail*. The key difference between sending mail to other AOL members and to people outside of AOL is how you address that mail. This page explains the basics of addressing and sending all three types of outside mail.

## TIP SHEET

▶ **You cannot unsend Internet, fax, or paper mail.**

▶ **You cannot attach files to Internet, fax, or paper mail, although AOL is working on providing you with the ability to attach files to Internet mail.**

▶ **You can send the same message to multiple Internet, fax, and paper-mail addresses. You can also mix and match AOL, Internet, and fax addresses. You cannot, however, mix and match paper-mail addresses with any other type of address.**

▶ **Your Internet address is your screen name in all lowercase characters, minus any spaces, followed by @aol.com. For example, if your screen name is *Kat Moran*, then your Internet address is *katmoran@aol.com*. For more information about the Internet, see Chapter 16.**

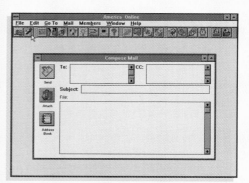

**1** Open a Compose Mail window as you normally would to start composing a mail message. (For details, refer back to "How to Send Mail to Another AOL Member" earlier in this chapter.) To send your message as Internet mail, continue on to step 2. To send your message as fax mail, skip to step 4. To send your message as paper mail, skip to step 6.

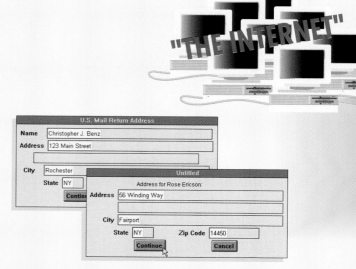

**8** A U.S. Mail Return Address dialog box opens, providing text boxes for your return address. Fill in these boxes as appropriate, and then click on Continue. Another dialog box opens, providing text boxes for your recipient's address. Fill in these boxes as appropriate, and then click on Continue again. A third dialog box then opens to inform you that your paper mail has been sent. (At least, it *will* be, within 24 hours.) Click on OK to close this third dialog box.

**7**  Unlike sending purely electronic mail, paper mail incurs an extra charge that will be billed to your AOL account. A dialog box opens to inform you of the charge. If this is acceptable, click on Yes.

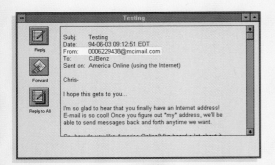

**3** Type your addressee's Internet address in the To list box, and then complete and send your message as you normally would for sending to another AOL member. Then you can skip the rest of this activity.

**2** Anyone whose e-mail system is connected to the Internet has a unique *Internet address*; it's similar to an AOL screen name. To determine a person's Internet address, ask for it. Or try having that person send you a message first, and then examine that message's From line to determine the return address.

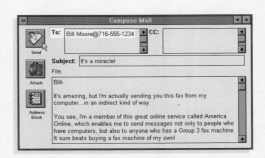

**4** To address your message as fax mail, type your addressee's name in the To list box, followed by @ and then the fax area code and telephone number. The addressee name (before the @) can be up to 20 characters long, including letters, numbers, and any punctuation marks except commas and parentheses. Then complete your message, sign on to AOL and bring the Compose Mail window to the front (if necessary), and click on Send.

**5** Unlike sending purely electronic mail, fax mail incurs an extra charge that will be billed to your AOL account. A dialog box opens to inform you of the charge. If this is acceptable, click on Yes. A second dialog box then opens to inform you that your fax mail has been sent. (At least, it *will* be, within the hour.) Click on OK to close the second dialog box, and then skip the rest of this activity.

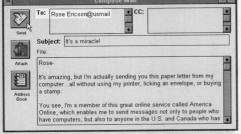

**6** To address your message as paper mail, type your addressee's name in the To list box, followed by @*usmail*. The addressee name (before the @) can be up to 33 characters long, including letters, numbers, and any punctuation marks except commas and parentheses. Then complete your message, sign on to AOL and bring the Compose Mail window to the front (if necessary), and click on Send.

# How to Use the Address Book

L ike postal addresses, *e-mail addresses* (AOL screen names, Internet addresses, and so on) can be difficult to remember. You could maintain a *paper* list of e-mail addresses as you would for postal addresses; a better option, though, is to take advantage of the AOL for Windows Address Book. The Address Book enables you to maintain an *electronic* list of your online correspondent's real names and e-mail addresses. In addition, the Address Book can help you easily and accurately address your mail messages.

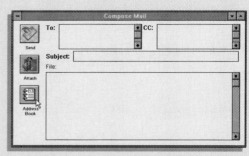

▶ **1** Open a Compose Mail window as you normally would to start composing a mail message. (For details, refer back to "How to Send Mail to Another AOL Member" earlier in this chapter.) Rather than typing an e-mail address in the To or CC list boxes, though, click on Address Book.

**8** Once you've added entries to the Address Book, you can use those entries to address future e-mail messages. To do so, open the Compose Mail window as you normally would, click on Address Book, click on the listed names and the To and/or CC buttons as desired, and then click on OK.

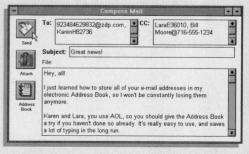

**7** Click on OK to return to your now-addressed mail message. Complete and send the message as you normally would.

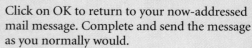

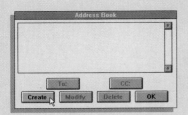

**2** An Address Book dialog box opens. To start creating an address entry, click on Create.

**3** An Address Group dialog box opens. In the Group Name text box, type your addressee's real name. In the Screen Names list box, type his or her e-mail address just as you would if you were typing it in the Compose Mail window's To or CC list box. This address can be an AOL, Internet, fax, or paper-mail address.

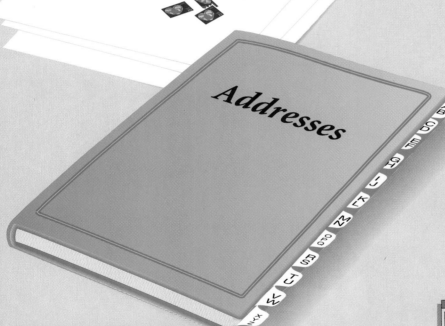

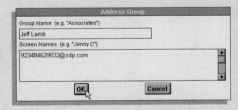

**4** Click on OK to add the entry to the Address Book.

**6** Now you can use the Address Book to address a mail message. Select the desired name, and then click on either To or CC. Clicking on To adds the corresponding e-mail address to the message's To list box; clicking on CC adds the address to the message's CC list box. To add multiple addresses to the message's To and/or CC list boxes, repeat this step as desired; the Address Book will automatically separate multiple addresses with the necessary commas.

**5** The Address Group dialog box closes, returning you to the Address Book dialog box, which now lists your acquaintance's real name as you typed it in the Group Name text box in step 3. To create additional addresses, repeat steps 2 through 4.

# TRY IT!

**H**ere's a hands-on opportunity to practice some of the many techniques involved in sending and receiving mail messages on AOL. You'll use much of of what you've learned in the previous chapter, as well as some important techniques from earlier chapters. Chapter numbers are included in parentheses after each step to show you where we first introduced the technique required to perform that step. (**Note:** Before attempting this activity, be sure that you have installed AOL for Windows and set up your AOL online membership account. For details, see Chapter 3.)

**1**

If necessary, switch on your computer and start Windows (Chapter 2).

**2**

Open the America Online program group and then double-click on the America Online program item to start AOL for Windows (Chapter 3).

**3**

Click on the Flashbar's Compose Mail icon to open the Compose Mail window (Chapter 7).

**4**

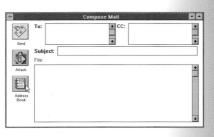

Click on Address Book to open the Address Book dialog box (Chapter 7).

**5**

Click on Create to open the Address Group dialog box (Chapter 7).

**6**

In the Group Name text box, type *your* real name (Chapter 7). Do not type the name shown here.

**7**

In the Screen Names list box, type *your* screen name (Chapter 7). Do not type the screen name shown here.

**8**

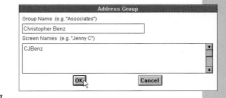

Click on OK to close the Address Group dialog box and return to the Address Book dialog box (Chapter 7).

**9**

Click on your name (if necessary), and then click on To (Chapter 7).

Continue to next page ▶

**TRY IT!**

Continue
below

Click on OK
to close the
Address
Book dialog
box and re-
turn to the
Compose Mail window (Chapter 7).

Verify that
your screen
name now
appears in
the Compose
Mail win-
dow's To list box. Then, in the Subject
text box, type **Practice** (Chapter 7).

In the
Compose
Mail win-
dow's central
list box, type
**I'm writing
to myself to practice sending and receiving electronic mail** (Chapter 7).

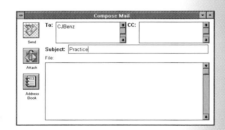

Choose Setup & Sign
On from the Go To
menu, to move the
Welcome window in
front of the Compose
Mail window
(Chapter 7).

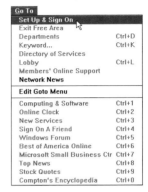

Verify that *your*
screen name dis-
plays in the
Screen Name
drop-down list
box. Then type
your password in
the Password text
box (Chapter 3).

Click on Sign On
(Chapter 3).

Wait a few
moments as
AOL for
Windows
dials your
local access
number, connects to AOL, checks your
password, and then opens the online
Welcome! window (Chapter 3).

**17**

Choose Compose Mail from the Window menu to move the Compose Mail window in front of the Welcome! window (Chapter 4).

**18**

Click on Send to send your e-mail message (Chapter 7).

**19**

Click on OK to close the dialog box that tells you your mail has been sent. (Chapter 7)

**20**

When the red flag on the Flashbar's Read New Mail icon comes up (which should be almost immediately), click on that icon to open the New Mail window (Chapter 7).

**21**

Verify that the message you just sent yourself is selected, and then click on Read (Chapter 7).

**22**

Examine the message, and then double-click on the message window's Control Menu box to close the message window (Chapter 2).

**23**

Choose Exit from the File menu (Chapter 3).

**24**

Click on Exit Application to both sign off from AOL and exit AOL for Windows (Chapter 3).

## CHAPTER 8

# Chatting

 As we mentioned at the beginning of Chapter 6, AOL is an electronic community comprising AOL's many members. In the past two chapters, you've seen two of the three primary ways to communicate with fellow members of this community: message boards and mail.

In this chapter, we'll show you a third way to communicate: *chatting*. Unlike message boards and mail, chatting is immediate, or *real-time*. Chatting is the electronic equivalent of a face-to-face or telephone conversation; there's virtually no lag time between sending a message and receiving a response.

So how does this chatting thing work? Well, anytime you're on line—even if it's in the middle of the night—you can be sure that there are other AOL members on line at the same time. To start chatting, you first enter one of AOL's many *chat rooms*. Once you're in a chat room, you type and send a message, and everyone in that room immediately sees that message. Because there can be up to 23 members in any one chat room, it's only a matter of seconds before you find yourself involved in a real-time conversation.

If you've never chatted on line before, it may seem somewhat strange at first, but do give it a try. Chatting is one of the best ways to meet new people, expose yourself to new ideas, and generally become more involved with your electronic community.

# How to Chat

AOL has dozens of different chat rooms. Most of them focus on a specific subject, but no matter what chat room you visit, the *techniques* for chatting are pretty much the same. If you're new to chatting, one of the best chat rooms to visit first is the Lobby, a chat room without any specific focus. Like a hotel lobby, AOL's Lobby is usually full of people going from one place to another, and a few are usually willing to linger a while and have a conversation. This page will show you how to visit the Lobby and how to chat.

**TIP SHEET**

▶ **In a roomful of people, it's easy to get lost in a sea of multiple conversations. Until you get used to chatting, be patient and try to stick to a single conversation.**

▶ **When you enter a chat room, you may be greeted by a person whose screen name starts with "Guide." This person is an *online guide*—a fellow member who volunteers to stay in a particular room, greet new entrants, and provide help as necessary. If you have any questions about chatting, ask your online guide.**

▶ **You may find that some chat messages include *online shorthands* such as ":)" and "LOL." (Online shorthands are also commonly used on message boards and in e-mail.) To learn more about online shorthands, click on PC Studio, double-click on What's Happening This Week, and then double-click on Online Shorthands.**

▶ **The Lobby is only one of AOL's many chat rooms. Visiting other chat rooms is covered later in this chapter.**

▶ **1** Make sure you're signed on to AOL, and then click on the Toolbar's People Connection icon. (Or choose Lobby from the Go To menu.)

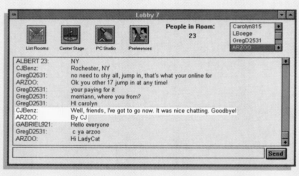

**8** When you're done chatting, be polite by sending out a good-bye message. Wait a few moments for other members' good-bye responses, and then close the Lobby window.

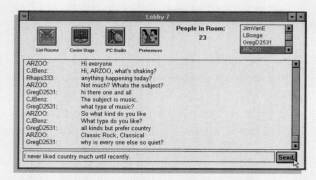

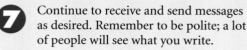

**7** Continue to receive and send messages as desired. Remember to be polite; a lot of people will see what you write.

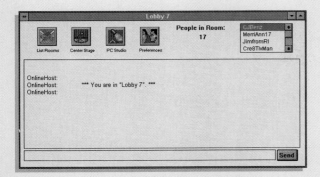

A Lobby window opens, and the automated OnlineHost greets you by telling you what Lobby you are in. If the original Lobby is full (23 members) you may find yourself in an alternate Lobby, such as Lobby 1, Lobby 2, and so on. No matter—every Lobby works the same.

**②**

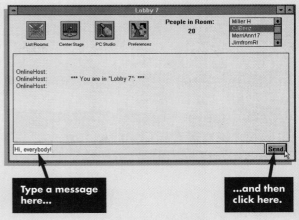

**Type a message here...**

**...and then click here.**

In the long text box at the bottom of the Lobby window, type a greeting message. Then click on Send. (As with messages on message boards and e-mail, avoid using uppercase—it's like shouting.)

**③**

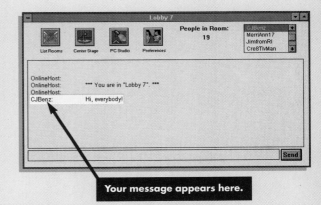

**Your message appears here.**

Your screen name appears in the window's central list box, followed by your message.

**④**

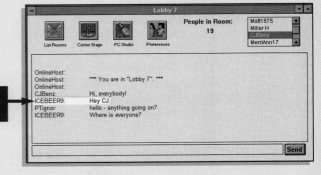

**A response quickly follows.**

Within seconds, you'll see someone else's message appear in the list box. They may be responding to you, sending out a general greeting, or talking to someone else. Keep in mind that you've just entered a roomful of people who may be already involved in a conversation.

**⑤**

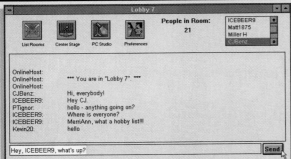

When someone responds to you, respond in turn by typing a message in that long text box, and then clicking on Send again. To indicate whom you're responding to (out of the possible 23 room occupants), be sure to include that member's screen name—or some abbreviation thereof—in your response. (Uppercase *is* acceptable when it's part of someone's screen name.)

**⑥**

# How to Share Personal Information with a Chat Partner

If you're like many people, you prefer to learn a little bit about another person before diving too deeply into a face-to-face *or* electronic conversation. But if you're starting an online conversation, it can take a lot of time to ask a person about his or her real name, hobbies, occupation, and so on. Enter the *member profile.* A member profile is an online personal-information form that many members fill out for use by other members. If your online chat partner has filled out a member profile, you can look at that profile to gain some insight into your partner. Ideally, you'll find some things you have in common; after all, isn't that how most friendships start?

## TIP SHEET

▶ You can share profiles in any chat room, not just the Lobby. You'll learn more about other chat rooms later in this chapter.

▶ You can also look up a member's profile by choosing Get a Member's Profile from the Members menu.

▶ Notice that the window shown in step 6 also provides a Message button. This button enables you to send an *Instant Message*—a chat message that only your recipient can see—to anyone in your current chat room. You can also send an Instant Message to almost anyone else who's currently on line, by choosing Send an Instant Message from the Members menu.

▶ If someone sends you an Instant Message, an Instant Message window will open automatically, showing you both the message and the sender's screen name. From this window, you can easily respond with an Instant Message of your own, by clicking on Respond in the Instant Message window.

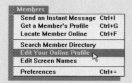

▶ **1** Before you start looking at other people's member profiles, it's polite first to complete one yourself. To fill out your own profile, make sure you're signed on to AOL, and then choose Edit Your Online Profile from the Members menu.

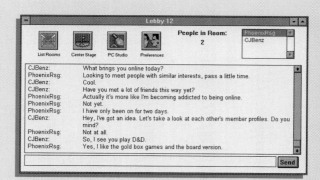

**8** Now you can talk about some of the things you have in common. It's a great way to start cementing your new friendship!

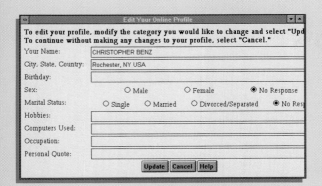

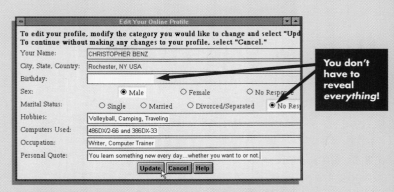

**2** The Edit Your Online Profile window opens, offering several text boxes and radio buttons that you can use to describe yourself. The Your Name and City, State, Country boxes are filled in for you already.

**3** You're not *required* to share personal information that you'd rather not reveal, so complete only those parts of your profile that you care to, and then click on Update.

**4** A dialog box informs you that your profile has been created. Click on OK to close this dialog box.

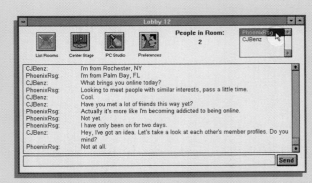

**5** Now that you've filled out your own profile, you can start looking at another person's profile with a clear conscience. To do so, move to the Lobby and start a conversation with someone. If you decide you'd like to learn more about your chat partner, invite your partner to take a moment to "share profiles." (You *can* peek at someone's profile secretly, but it's much more fun to *share* profiles.) To see a profile, find and double-click on the person's screen name in the list box in the Lobby window's upper-right corner.

**7** If the person has filled out a member profile, that profile will display in a Member Profile window. (If he or she hasn't filled out a member profile, a dialog box informs you that no profile is available.) Read the profile, and then return to the Lobby; your chat partner should arrive back at about the same time.

**6** A window bearing that person's screen name opens. Click on Get Info.

# How to Visit Other Chat Rooms

When you visit the Lobby, you've actually stepped into the entranceway of AOL's People Connection department, which is entirely dedicated to chatting. From within the Lobby, you can visit just about any other chat room. AOL's chat rooms fall into three categories: *public rooms*, which are permanent rooms that AOL has set up to address a variety of member interests; *member rooms*, which are temporary public rooms that members create to discuss a topic not addressed by an existing public room; and *private rooms*, which are temporary rooms that members create to discuss topics privately.

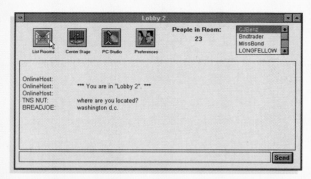

▶ **1** Go to the Lobby (see "How to Chat" earlier in this chapter), and then click on List Rooms.

**8** When you want to move from your new room to another room, click once again on the List Rooms button.

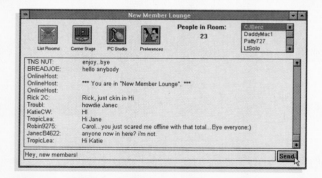

**7** Regardless of what type of room you enter, the automated OnlineHost greets you by telling you what room you are in. Your new room window probably looks and works exactly as it did in the Lobby; you may even see some leftover Lobby conversation. Once you've arrived in a room, introduce yourself and start chatting, just as you would if you were in the Lobby. Remember, though, that if your new room has a specific focus, you should try to stick to the topic at hand.

**TIP SHEET**

▶ **You can't visit a room that's already filled to its 23-member capacity—at least, not until someone leaves.**

▶ **If you still can't find a room to suit you, try creating your *own* room. To do so, click on Create Room or Private Room (where available), provide a name for your room, and then click on Create or Go. Rooms you create through the Create Room button will automatically appear in the Member Rooms window, and anyone can visit. Rooms created through the Private Room button, however, are more restricted; only those members who know when and under what name your private room exists can join you there.**

▶ **If you're a parent who wants to let one of your children share your AOL account, you may be concerned about the focus of certain chat rooms, especially those created by other members. Fortunately, you can prevent your children from visiting certain rooms. See Chapter 11 to learn how.**

**2** An Active Public Rooms window opens, listing every *active* public room—that is, every public room that currently contains members. To visit 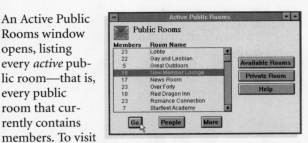 an active public room, scroll through the list box until you find a room that interests you, click on that room, click on Go, and then skip to step 7. (If the More button is active, you can use this button to add more active public rooms to the list.) To check out other room options instead, continue on to step 3.

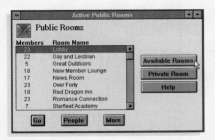

**3** Click on Available Rooms.

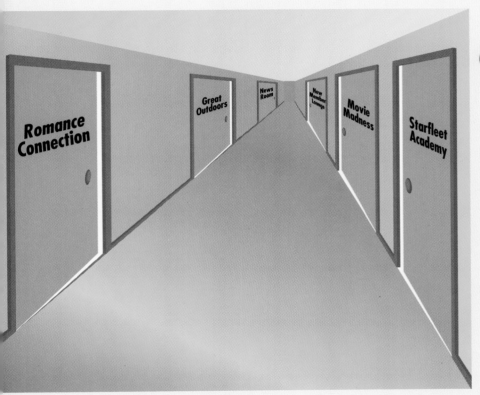

**4** The Available Rooms window opens, listing every available public room— that is, every public room that's cur-  rently empty. To visit an empty public room (thus making it an *active* public room), scroll through the list box until you find a room that interests you, click on that room, click on Open, and then skip to step 7. (If the More button is active, you can use this button to add more available public rooms to the list.) To check out other room options instead, continue on to step 5.

**5** Click on Member Rooms.

**6** The Member Rooms window opens, listing every available member room. To visit a member room, scroll through the list box until you find a room that interests you, click on that room, click on Open, and then continue on to step 7. (If the More button is active, you can use this button to add more available public rooms to the list.)

# How to Find Out about Upcoming Events

**A**s you explore AOL's public chat rooms, you may find it hard to determine the purpose of certain rooms. If you visit the Great Outdoors room, for example, you may only find a few people chatting, and they may be discussing anything *but* the Great Outdoors. This is because many of AOL's public rooms, much like hotel conference rooms, are event-oriented. Visit a hotel conference room between events, and the room seems purposeless; the same is true of AOL's public rooms. This page shows some ways to find out about AOL's *online events*.

▶ **1** Go to the Lobby or to any other People Connection chat room, and then click on PC Studio.

## TIP SHEET

▸ **The options we've shown you here generally provide information only on regularly scheduled, general-interest events. For other types of events, explore some of the other options listed in the What's Happening This Week window.**

▸ **For all the exploring you do through the What's Happening This Week window, you'll still learn mostly about events in the People Connection department. To learn about events in other departments, use the keyword *titf*.**

▸ **The Welcome! window that opens when you sign on to AOL, and the Goodbye From America Online! window that opens when you sign off without exiting AOL for Windows, often display advertisements for current or upcoming events.**

▸ **Because of their overwhelming popularity, some events are held in special rooms called *auditoriums*, which are capable of holding more than 23 people at one time. Two such auditoriums are Center Stage (keyword *center stage*) and the Rotunda (keyword *rotunda*). Visit these areas to see their own specific listings of upcoming events.**

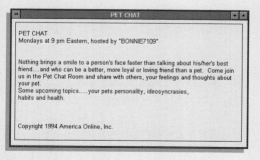

**8** A new window opens, containing a description of your chosen event.

**2** The PC Studio window opens. Click on What's Happening This Week (if necessary), and then click on Open.

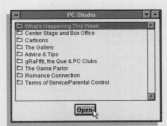

**3** The What's Happening This Week window opens. To see the schedule of upcoming general events, click on Event Rooms Schedule (if necessary), and then click on Open.

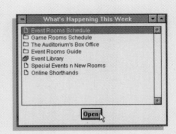

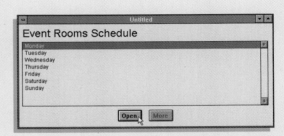

**4** Another window opens, listing every day of the week. Click on the day you'd like to attend an event (if necessary), and then click on Open.

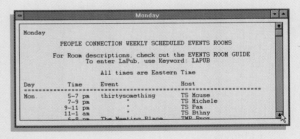

**5** The next window lists your chosen day's events. Each listing includes a time, the event/room name, and the screen name of that event's online host or hosts. (An *online host*—not to be confused with the automated OnlineHost—is a live person who moderates events.

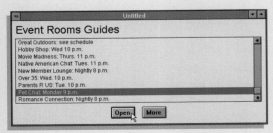

**6** To learn more about the event you plan to attend, return to the What's Happening This Week window, click on Event Rooms Guide, and then click on Open.

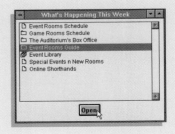

**7** An Event Rooms Guide window opens, listing events in alphabetical order. Scroll to find the desired event (using the More button as necessary), click on that event, and then click on Open.

# CHAPTER 9

# Searchable Databases

 We've already mentioned searchable databases several times throughout this book. In Chapter 4, we introduced you to the very basics of working with a searchable database called the Directory of Services. In Chapter 5, you learned that AOL's Top News area features a searchable database of news articles, and that many online magazines feature searchable databases. In Chapter 7, we told you that you can find another member's screen name by using yet another searchable database, the Member Directory.

Clearly, the searchable database is a pretty common AOL feature. But what *is* a searchable database, and how do you search one?

A *database* is simply a collection of related information, and electronic databases are quite common in the computer world. How you search a searchable database depends both on the database and on the information you're trying to find. The basic search techniques, however, are common among all AOL searchable databases and among all searches. This chapter will show you those techniques.

# How to Search a Searchable Database

In Chapter 4, you learned the fundamentals of searching a searchable database: You type a search criterion, and then click on List Articles for a list of articles that meet your criterion. This type of basic search works well in some circumstances, but isn't very efficient in others. For example, if you search AOL's News Search database using the criterion "politics," AOL might list hundreds of articles. In cases like this, you'll want to narrow your search and get a much shorter, more precise list—by using a more specific criterion and/or by specifying multiple criteria. This page shows you how.

## TIP SHEET

▶ **If no List Articles button is available, click on whatever appropriately named button *is* available.**

▶ **The word *and* is only one of three available multiple search tools; the other two are *or* and *not*. Use *or* to broaden your search to items that match *any* criteria; use *not* to reverse your search to articles that *don't* match a criterion. For example, *dogs or cats* would find articles about dogs, about cats, or about both; *dogs not cats* would find articles about dogs, unless the articles were also about cats.**

▶ **You can mix and match search tools freely, but your total search phrase cannot exceed 45 characters, including spaces.**

▶ **Before searching a database, consider clicking on the search window's Help & Info button to get information specific to that database. For example, by clicking on the Movie & Video Database window's Help & Info button, you will see that you can search for G-rated movies by using the criterion *MPAAG*.**

**1** Searchable databases are available all over AOL. For central access to these databases, however, proceed directly to AOL's Reference Desk. To move to the Reference Desk, use the keyword **reference**. (Or click on the Flashbar's Learning & Reference icon, and then on The Reference Desk.)

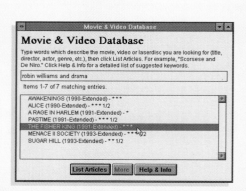

**8** Once the list is down to a manageable size, double-click on any article that interests you.

**7** If your multiple criteria produces the short list you need, skip to step 8. If your list is still too long, repeat steps 5 and/or 6, using additional or more-specific criteria. If your criteria has narrowed your search *too* much, however, a dialog box like this one will tell you that no matches have been found. Click on OK to close the dialog box, and then repeat steps 5 and/or 6 using *less*-specific criteria and *fewer* total criteria.

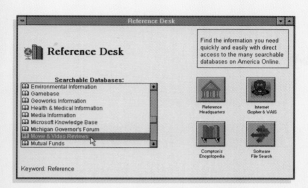

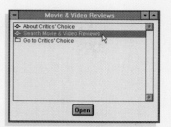

**2** The Reference Desk window opens, providing a lengthy list of searchable databases. Scroll through the list until you find a database that interests you, and then double-click on that database.

**3** If the next window that opens looks similar to the search window pictured in step 4, then skip to step 4. Otherwise, you may get a window or a series of windows like this one, which gives you some more choices along the way. Double-click on the likeliest choice in each window (usually any choice that includes the word *search*) until a search window opens (see the one pictured in step 4).

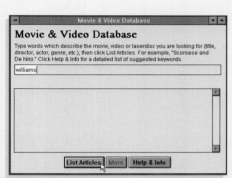

**4** It's usually best to start out with a fairly general criterion first, just to see how many items are available within that general area. Type that criterion in the text box at the top of the search window, and then click on List Articles.

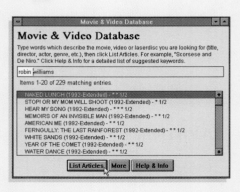

**6** If your more-specific criterion produces a list that is short enough for you, skip to step 8. Otherwise, repeat step 5 using an even more specific criterion—or consider using multiple criteria. To use multiple criteria, type in two or more individual criterion separated by the word *and*. Then, click again on List Articles.

**5** If your general criterion produces a short list, then skip to step 8. Otherwise, narrow your search. Type a more specific criterion, and then click again on List Articles.

# CHAPTER 10

# Help!

Confused? Lost? Just plain stuck?

Relax. No matter how many books you read or how much computer experience you have, you're bound to need some help with AOL now and then. Knowing this, AOL provides easily accessible help in two forms: *online help* and *offline help*.

Online help is stored on AOL's computers in Virginia, and there's plenty of it. You can get up-to-date, ready-to-use help for just about any AOL question you have. For example, you can find out how to make AOL for Windows run better on your computer, how to determine an Internet address, how to find a specific area within AOL, or how to locate online job listings. As an added bonus, you can do all this for free because using online help incurs *no online charges*!

Unfortunately, online help has no value if what you need is help to get online in the first place. That's where offline help comes in handy. Offline help is stored on your own computer's hard drive, so it's accessible whether or not you're signed on to AOL. Like online help, offline help is also free to use—that is, as long as you use it off line.

This chapter introduces you to the wonderful worlds of offline and online help.

# How to Get Offline Help

**W**hy won't my new modem dial when I click on Sign On? How can I connect to AOL when I'm away from home? How can I change my local access numbers? Can I get my modem to stop making those annoying sounds when I first sign on? The answers to these and many more questions are waiting for you in offline help.

**► 1** Start AOL for Windows, but don't sign on to AOL. (If you *can* sign on, you might as well skip right to the next page to learn about online help.) Then choose Contents from the Help menu.

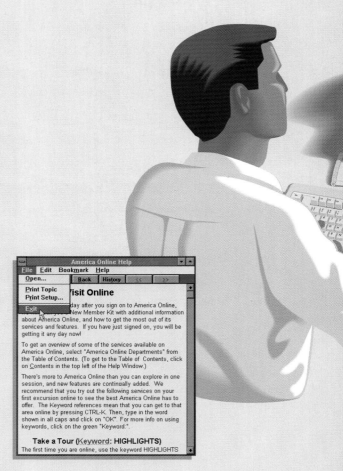

**TIP SHEET**

▶ **Another convenient way to get offline help is to** *search* **for help much as you would search a searchable database (see Chapter 9). To start searching for help, choose Search for Help On, in the AOL for Windows Help menu, or click on Search in the America Online Help window.**

▶ **To get offline help on using offline help, choose How to Use Help from any Help menu.**

▶ **If you can't find the help you need in offline help, and you aren't able to sign on to AOL, you still have at least two other options: You can call AOL by telephone at 1-800-827-6364, or you can use another communications program (such as Windows Terminal) to call AOL's Technical Support BBS (bulletin board system) by modem at 1-800-827-5808.**

▶ **When using offline help, bear in mind that some of the information may be out of date. For the most current information, double-check with online help, if possible (see next page).**

**8** Note that the America Online Help window has its own menu bar, separate from the AOL for Windows menu bar. When you're done with help and you want to return to AOL for Windows, choose Exit from the File menu in the America Online Help window.

**2** The America Online Help application window opens, listing available help topics. (Your Help window may look different from this one.)

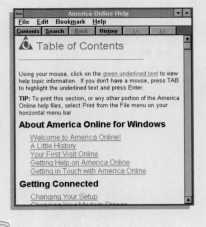

**3** Every help topic has a solid underline. Scroll to find an appropriate topic, and then click on it. (As you point to a topic, notice that the mouse pointer changes to a pointing hand.)

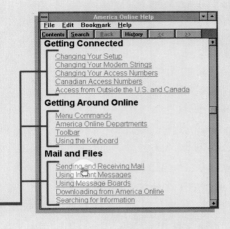

**Topics**

How may I help you?

OFFLINE HELP

**4** A new help screen appears, displaying information on your selected topic. Scroll to read the topic. If this help screen, too, displays solid-underlined topics, click on those topics as desired to jump to other help screens.

**More topics**

**6** Sometimes you'll come across a word or phrase with a dotted underline. To see a definition of that word or phrase, click on it; a box containing the definition opens. Once you've read the definition, click on the box to close it.

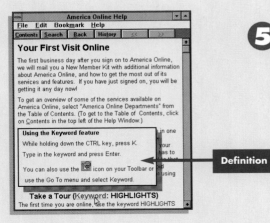

**Definition**

**5** To return to a previous help screen, click on Back.

**7** Continue clicking, scrolling, and reading until you have the information you need.

# How to Get Online Help

Like offline help, AOL's online help provides screen after screen of useful solutions. Online help, though, takes help one step further. You see, if you have a problem or question for which AOL has no ready answer, you still have *three* additional online methods for finding a solution: by chatting live with AOL's Customer Service technicians, by sending an e-mail to Customer Relations, or by presenting your problem to fellow AOL members through a message board. Between all the prepared solutions and these three live resources, you'll be able to solve just about any AOL problem.

## TIP SHEET

▶ **Members' Online Support isn't the only place to find online help. Almost everywhere you go on AOL, you'll find various buttons, list-box items, and online guides that will provide help and information on the current area. Although getting help this way isn't free, it *can* be a lot more convenient.**

▶ **You cannot send or receive Instant Messages (see Chapter 8) when you're in a free area. You will, however, be notified of new mail.**

▶ **Don't wait until you have a problem to explore online help; it's good to know how to get help *before* you need it. Besides, in addition to solutions to specific problems, online help also suggests methods for using AOL more fully and efficiently.**

▶ **Three of the features we've described earlier in this book—the Directory of Services, keyword lists, and your member profile—can be accessed through online help without charge. Explore online help to see how.**

▶ **1** Make sure you're signed on to AOL, then choose Members' Online Support from the Go To menu.

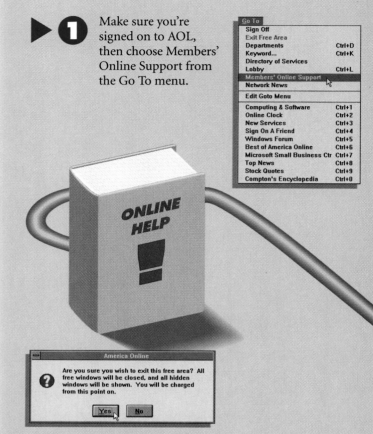

**8** Once you've found your solution, or at least left a message asking for one, choose Exit Free Area from the Go To menu. A dialog box informs you that your online time charges will resume. Click on Yes to continue; any windows that were hidden when you entered the free area will reappear.

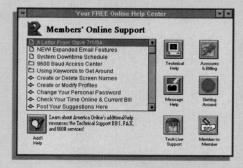

**7** If you can't find the answer you need, return to Your FREE Online Help Center, and then click on either Tech Live Support or Member to Member. Tech Live Support enables you to chat with AOL's Customer Service technicians. Member to Member enables you to send an e-mail to AOL's Customer Relations department or takes you to a message board dedicated to problem solving among AOL members.

**2** A dialog box informs you that you're about to enter a free area. This dialog box also warns that certain windows will be closed, or temporarily hidden, until you leave the free area. Click on Yes to continue.

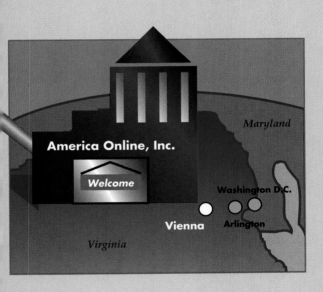

**3** Next, you'll see Your FREE Online Help Center. As soon as this window appears, you can take a moment and relax, knowing that you're no longer being charged for your online time.

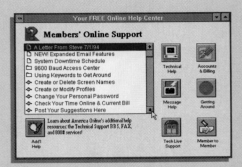

**4** Scroll through the list box to see if anything there can help you with your problem. If you find something, double-click on it and continue from there. Otherwise, continue on to step 5.

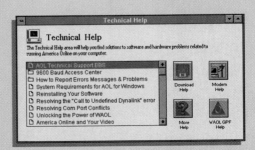

**6** All the buttons mentioned in step 5 take you to a specialized help window such as this one. From here, double-click on list-box items and/or click on buttons until you arrive at a window that displays the prepared solution you need.

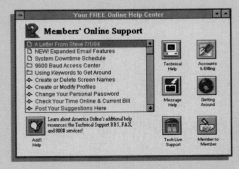

**5** If your problem is related to running AOL for Windows on your computer, click on the Technical Help button. If you have a question about online charges or if you want to change your account information, click on Accounts & Billing. For help with using message boards, e-mail, or chat rooms, click on Message Help. To find out about various AOL services, click on Getting Around.

## CHAPTER 11

# For Parents Only

For many families these days, the home computer is a multi-purpose tool. Mom and Dad use it for tracking the family budget and calculating income taxes, the kids spend their computer time doing homework and playing games, and everyone uses the computer to type up personal letters.

As an extension of your computer, AOL also serves a variety of family purposes. Some AOL features, such as stock quotes and airline reservations, appeal primarily to adults. Other features, such as homework help and games, are geared more toward kids. And many features can be equally enjoyed by all, such as e-mail and online magazines. These next two chapters focus on ways to use AOL as a shared family resource.

This chapter is a guide for parents who want to introduce their family to AOL. It shows parents how to share a single AOL membership account among family members, how to get a parent's-eye view of AOL through the Parents' System Map, and how to control kids' access to certain AOL areas. Chapter 12 takes a closer look at a couple of selected AOL features that your kids might want to check out.

# How to Share AOL with Your Family

There are several ways you *could* share your AOL account with your family. You could let them use your existing screen name and password, but then any one of them could receive (and even accidentally delete!) your mail, send out messages bearing your name, and so on. You could also get a separate membership account for each family member, but the combined monthly membership fees could really add up. The best way to share your existing AOL membership account is by establishing up to four *subaccounts*—each with a unique screen name and password—under your single account, and still pay the same monthly membership fee. This page shows you how.

## TIP SHEET

▶ For the most part, subaccounts act as separate membership accounts, complete with their own e-mail addresses and member profiles.

▶ To make each subaccount's password private, set generic passwords at first, and then have family members sign on and change their passwords individually. To start changing a password, double-click on Change Your Personal Password in the Your FREE Online Help Center window's central list box.

▶ Make sure that every family member who shares your account is familiar with AOL's online rules, or *terms of service*. As the *master account holder*, you are responsible for all subaccounts. To learn about AOL's terms of service, sign on and use the keyword *tos*.

▶ To start deleting a screen name, double-click on Delete a Screen Name in the Delete Screen Names window shown in step 2. You can delete any screen name except your original one, and you can only delete screen names through the master account.

▶ **1** Before signing on to AOL, ask each family member to provide a list of suggested screen names for his or her subaccount. Like your own screen name, your family's screen names can be 3 to 10 characters long, including spaces. Because each screen name must be unique to AOL, explain to your family that they may not be able to get *exactly* the screen names they want. Then, sign on to AOL, open Your FREE Online Help Center (see Chapter 10 for details), and double-click on Create or Delete Screen Names in the window's list box.

Click here for a list of screen names.

**8** To sign on to AOL with one of the new screen names, open the Screen Name drop-down list box in either the Welcome window or the Goodbye from America Online! window, click on the desired screen name, type the appropriate password in the Password text box, and then click on Sign On.

**7** Repeat steps 2–6 for each additional screen name, and then sign off.

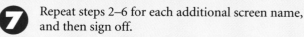

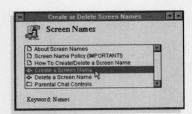

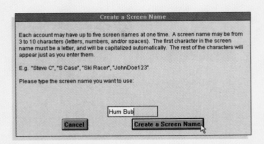

**2** The Create or Delete Screen Names window opens. Double-click on Create a Screen Name.

**3** The Create a Screen Name dialog box opens. In the text box near the bottom of the window, type a screen name for the first subaccount, and then click on Create a Screen Name.

**4** If the screen name you typed in step 3 is unique to AOL, then the Set Password dialog box shown in step 5 opens. Otherwise, AOL will ask you to try other screen names until you either provide a unique screen name or accept one that AOL suggests. (The screen name that AOL suggests is usually a variation of the name you typed, followed by a string of numbers.)

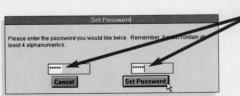

Type the *same* password in both boxes.

**6** If all is well, a dialog box opens to inform you that the screen name has been added to your account. Click on OK to close this dialog box.

**5** Type a password for the new screen name in each of the two text boxes. Like your own screen name's password, this password can be 4 to 8 characters long, and should be something that's easily remembered but not easily guessed. (To be safe, write down the password.) For security reasons, the password will display on screen as asterisks. When you're done, click on Set Password.

# How to Use the Parents' System Map

If you're like many parents, you want your kids' experience with computers to be fun, but also educational. So if you've established AOL subaccounts for your kids, you now face the task of determining which AOL areas are appropriately entertaining and/or educational. To make this task easier, AOL offers an online Parents' System Map, which serves as your guide to AOL features for children. By investing 15 to 30 minutes with the Map, you'll glean dozens of ideas for making the most of your kids' online time. This page shows you how to get started with the Map.

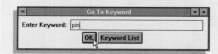

▶ **1** Make sure you're signed on to AOL, and then use the keyword *pin* or *parent*. (Or click on the Flashbar's Learning & Reference icon, and then double-click on Parents' Information Network.)

**TIP SHEET**

▶ Don't expect online learning to be automatic. To enhance the learning experience, be sure to monitor your kids' online sessions on a regular basis, providing assistance and suggestions when appropriate.

▶ As with any communications medium (television, telephone, and so on), try to limit your kids' daily AOL usage. Unlimited online time can result not only in hefty online charges, but it can also prevent your kids from enjoying other activities of a healthy childhood. Moderation is the key.

▶ As you may have noticed, the Parents' System Map is only one part of a larger AOL feature called the Parents' Information Network (PIN). This network is more than just a guide to other AOL areas; it's a major resource for parents. The PIN offers a wealth of information on a wide range of parenting issues, and serves as a communication conduit among parents and education specialists.

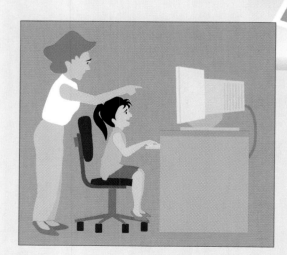

**7** Once you've collected and organized a list of paths and keywords, go ahead and explore those areas on your own, just to make sure they provide the level of entertainment and education you expected. Then sit down with each of your kids individually, give them your hand-picked list of keywords and paths, and teach them the basics of signing on, using keywords and paths, and signing off.

**2** The Parents'
Information
Network win-
dow opens. At
the bottom of
this window,
click on Parents'
System Map.

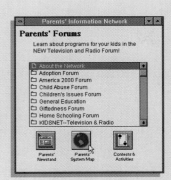

**3** The Parents' System
Map window opens,
listing most of AOL's
departments, as well as
some additional areas
designed especially for
parents and kids. Click
on one of the listed
departments, and then
click on Open.

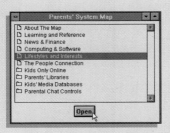

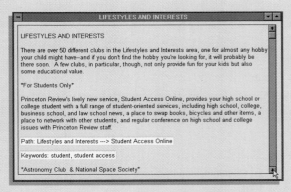

**4** A department window opens, describing areas
within that department that may be appropriate for your kids. Like the Directory of Services
(see Chapter 4), each area description also includes a path and keywords for moving to that
area. Scroll through the descriptions, and when
you find an area of interest, note the area's path
and/or keywords.

**6** From the Parents' System
Map window, you may
also want to explore some
of the areas designed especially for parents or kids.
Kids Only Online (KOOL)
is an "electronic fun-
house" where kids aged 5
through 14 can practice

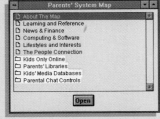

**5** Close the current department window, and then repeat steps 3 and 4
as desired for each of the other
listed departments.

communicating with one another and with education specialists
via closely monitored message boards and chat rooms. The
Parents' Libraries area helps parents find software for their children. And the Kids' Media Databases area provides access to
searchable databases of educational magazines and television and
radio shows. (You'll learn about Parental Chat Controls on the
next page.)

# How to Set Up Parental Controls

Once you've explored the Parents' System Map, you'll realize that AOL can be a valuable part of your childrens' education. As in any community, though, AOL's electronic community may provide learning opportunities that you don't want your kids to experience. One of these is the use of foul, abusive, or suggestive language in unmonitored chat rooms or in Instant Messages. Although AOL expressly forbids such language, it does sometimes occur. If this concerns you, you may want to set up *parental controls* on any or all of your children's subaccounts to prevent them from visiting certain chat rooms and/or receiving Instant Messages. Here's how.

## TIP SHEET

▶ **Although parental controls can prevent your kids from using features that are especially prone to member abuse, these controls are not a panacea. Also, they can interfere with some appropriately educational AOL features (see Chapter 12). The best way to help your kids enjoy AOL in the most productive way is to monitor their online sessions.**

▶ **As an alternative to parental controls, you might want to guide your kids to rooms that are carefully monitored by AOL staff or volunteers, such as KOOL's Tree House or People Connection's Teen Chat room.**

▶ **If you or your family *do* encounter inappropriate language or any other terms-of-service violations in a People Connection chat room, use the keyword *guide pager*; within minutes, an AOL representative will assist you. To report violations in other areas, use the keyword *tos*, and then click on Write to Terms of Service Staff. Include as many details as possible, including where you encountered the violation and the offender's screen name.**

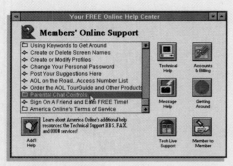

▶ **1** Sign on to AOL using the master account, open Your FREE Online Help Center (see Chapter 10 for details), scroll down in the window's list box, and double-click on Parental Chat Controls. (You can also access Parental Chat Controls from the Parents' System Map window shown on the previous page, but access through Your FREE Online Help Center is free; access through the Parents' System Map window is not.)

**8** Should a family member attempt to use a feature that you've blocked from his or her account, this dialog box will say that the feature is blocked.

**7** A dialog box informs you that your controls have been saved. Click on OK to close this dialog box.

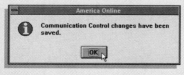

**2** The Parental Chat Controls window opens. Click on Parental Control (if necessary), and then click on Open.

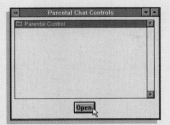

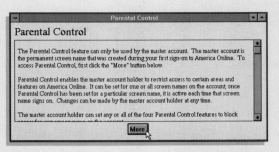

**3** A Parental Control window opens, describing how to set parental controls. Read this information if you'd like, and then click on More.

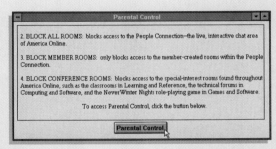

**4** A second Parental Control window opens, displaying more information about parental controls. Read this information if you'd like, and then click on Parental Control.

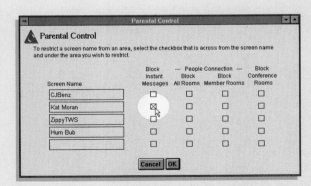

**5** A third (and final!) Parental Control window opens, displaying every screen name on your account. To set controls on any or all of these subaccounts, check the corresponding check boxes as needed. Block Instant Messages prevents the receipt or sending of Instant Messages; Block All Rooms prevents entrance to *any* People Connection chat room; Block Member Rooms prevents entrance to any member-created People Connection chat room; and Block Conference Rooms prevents entrance to any chat room *outside* the People Connection department.

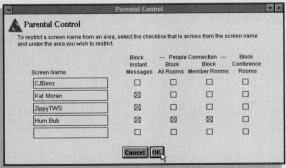

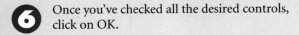

**6** Once you've checked all the desired controls, click on OK.

# CHAPTER 12

# Kids

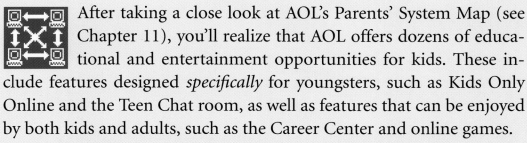 After taking a close look at AOL's Parents' System Map (see Chapter 11), you'll realize that AOL offers dozens of educational and entertainment opportunities for kids. These include features designed *specifically* for youngsters, such as Kids Only Online and the Teen Chat room, as well as features that can be enjoyed by both kids and adults, such as the Career Center and online games.

Because AOL has so much to offer to young people, and because the range of features expands almost constantly, we can't expect to cover all or even most of them in one thin chapter. So we'll do our best to introduce you to AOL's most responsive *educational* feature, the Teacher Pager; and arguably its most prominent *entertainment* feature, online games. These two features alone can keep your kids busy for hours on end. And with any luck, you and your kids will get enough of a taste of AOL that you'll want to explore additional features on your own.

**Note:** Except for this introductory page, this chapter is addressed primarily to the kids who will actually be performing the steps shown. If your family is new to AOL, you'll want to familiarize yourself with the next two pages, and then help your kids work through the steps, providing explanations where appropriate.

# How to Get Live Homework Help

**H**omework can be a real chore. Sometimes the assignment seems boring; other times it's hard to understand. You *could* ask your parents for help, but you may have found that they don't always know the answers. So who else can you ask for help? Well, who better to help you with homework than a teacher? Through AOL's *Teacher Pager*, you can chat online with a teacher—sometimes within minutes after you sign on. Whether the subject is arithmetic or astronomy, zoology or Zagreb, one of AOL's knowledgeable online teachers can guide you, one-on-one and step-by-step, toward solving all your homework problems.

## TIP SHEET

- ▶ In general, use the Teacher Pager only when you need help within 48 hours. Other ways to get homework help include visiting the IES Help Room to see if a teacher is already there; dropping in on regularly scheduled help sessions; signing up for individual tutoring sessions; and posting your question on one of the AAC's message boards. Explore the items listed in the AAC window (shown in step 2) to learn more about these alternatives.

- ▶ If you can't make your appointment, be sure to cancel it by sending the message "Please Cancel My Appointment" through the Teacher Pager.

- ▶ Besides homework help, the AAC also offers help with term papers, help with exams, an online encyclopedia, and much, much more.

- ▶ If your parents have set up Parental Controls for you, you may not be able to chat with any teachers. If you need homework help, ask your parents to remove these controls for at least a little while.

▶**1** Make sure you're signed on to AOL, and then use the keyword **homework** or **tutoring**. (Or click on the Flashbar's Learning & Reference icon, and then double-click on Academic Assistance Center.)

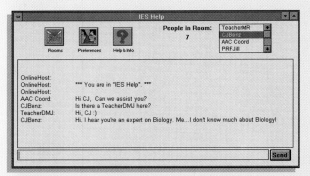

**8** You'll eventually meet with a teacher in a chat room. This usually is the IES (Interactive Education Services) Help Room—also known as the Homework Help Room—which you can enter by clicking on Homework Help Room in the AAC window shown in step 2. If the meeting room is someplace else, then the coordinator or your assigned teacher will tell you the name of that room and give you instructions for getting there.

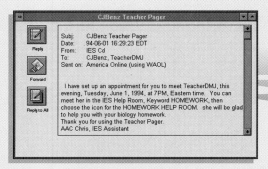

**7** If you *don't* receive an Instant Message within two minutes, then the coordinator is either off duty or too busy to answer your page right now. Sign off, and then check your e-mail later. The coordinator will send you an e-mail message—usually within a few hours—telling you when and where a teacher will be able to meet with you.

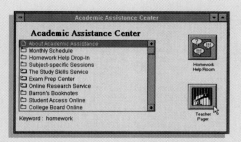

**2** The Academic Assistance Center (AAC) window opens. Click on Teacher Pager.

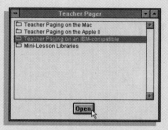

**3** A Teacher Pager window opens. Click on Teacher Paging on an IBM-compatible, and then click on Open.

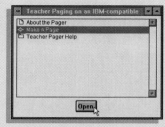

**4** The Teacher Paging on an IBM-Compatible window opens. Click on Make A Page, and then click on Open.

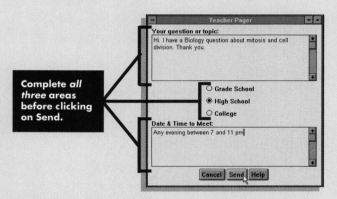

Complete *all three* areas before clicking on Send.

**5** A second Teacher Pager window opens. In the window's top text box, describe your homework problem in as much detail as possible. Between the text boxes, click on the option that best describes what grade you're in. In the bottom text box, type some dates and times when you can meet on line with a teacher, just in case a teacher isn't available right away. Finally, click on Send, and then click on OK to close the next dialog box.

**6** Your *teacher page* is sent to a coordinator, who will read your question and decide which teachers are available to answer your question. Stay on line for a minute or two to give the coordinator a chance to reply to your page; feel free to explore any other AOL area (except a free area) while you wait. If all goes well, you'll receive an Instant Message within a couple of minutes telling you how to go on from there. Generally, the message will indicate that help is available right now, or that the coordinator is still looking for an available teacher.

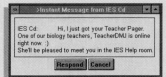

# How to Find Out about Online Games

B eing a kid isn't just about going to school, doing your homework, and finishing your chores; it's also about having fun *playing games.* AOL knows this, and has dozens of different games that you can play on line. Most of these games are *parlor games* (games that you play in a chat room with other AOL members). AOL's parlor games include word games, number games, music games, and trivia games. Some games even offer free online time as prizes. We can't possibly show you how to play all these games on one page, but we *will* show you where to go to find out more about the games that interest you most.

## TIP SHEET

▶ **Games aren't just for kids. Invite your parents to play online games with you.**

▶ **If your parents have set up Parental Controls for you, you may not be able to play any online games. Try to convince them that the games are educational (they are!), and to remove these controls for at least a little while.**

▶ **To learn about other online games, visit AOL's Games & Entertainment department. (Click on the Toolbar's Games & Entertainment icon or use the keyword *games*.) The games in this department include Neverwinter Nights, a role-playing adventure game, and RabbitJack's Casino, a gambling casino featuring poker, blackjack, and more. Unlike parlor games, though, these games require that you first obtain and set up special game software.**

▶ **Besides *online* games, you can download any one of AOL's thousands of *offline* games—games you can play without being signed on. For details on downloading games, see Chapter 15.**

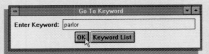

**1** Most of AOL's parlor games are in AOL's People Connection department. To learn more about these games, first make sure you're signed on to AOL, and then use the keyword **parlor.**

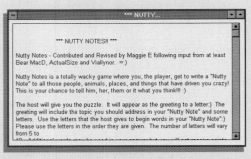

**7** A window opens, displaying a description of your chosen game and its rules.

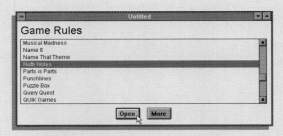

**6** The Game Rules window opens. Use the scroll bar and More button as necessary to find the game you want, click on that game, and then click on Open.

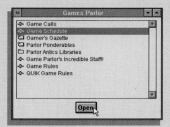

**2** The Games Parlor window opens. Click on Game Schedule, and then click on Open.

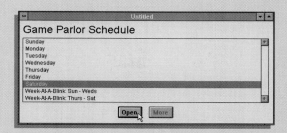

**3** The Game Parlor Schedule window opens. Click on the day or the Week-At-A-Blink set of days that you're available to play online games, and then click on Open.

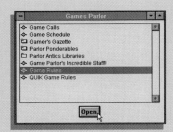

**5** To learn the rules of a particular game before you play, return to the Games Parlor window, click on Game Rules, and then click on Open.

**4** A window opens to show you the People Connection games scheduled for the day or days you chose. Scroll through this window, making notes about the games that sound interesting, and when and where they'll take place. (If you're interested in a lot of games, you can save or print the schedule, instead.) Then you can sign on and visit these chat rooms at the scheduled times. (Chapter 8 shows you how to visit chat rooms.)

## CHAPTER 13

# Traveling with America Online

 Whether it's for business or pleasure, travel can be hard work. Even before you leave home, you need to choose a destination, plan an itinerary, draft a travel budget, and make all the necessary reservations.

Fortunately, AOL can help simplify some of these details. Wherever you're going—a business trip to Raleigh, a family vacation to Disney World, or a weekend getaway to Toronto—AOL can help you get there and enjoy yourself once you arrive. This chapter introduces you to two AOL features devoted entirely to travel: EAAsy Sabre and Travelers' Corner.

Think of EAAsy Sabre as your online travel agent. This comprehensive reservation system is the same one used by over 10,000 travel agencies. It enables you to research and even reserve airline flights, hotel rooms, and rental cars, directly from your own computer. (Although EAAsy Sabre is owned and operated by American Airlines—thus the *AA* in E*AA*sy Sabre—the system manages information on the flights of over 600 airlines worldwide.)

If EAAsy Sabre is your online travel *agent*, then Travelers' Corner is your online travel *advisor*. Use it to choose an exciting destination or to learn more about a destination you've already selected. Whether your travel plans take you across the country or around the world, Travelers' Corner stands ready with valuable and insightful information.

So the next time you're planning a trip, let AOL help you with your travel plans. Once you do, travel won't seem like such hard work after all!

# How to Use EAAsy Sabre

If you've ever visited a travel agency in person, you've probably seen the clunky computer terminals that travel agents use to research and book airline flights and other travel reservations. Those terminals—and thousands like them— are all connected to EAAsy Sabre, a mammoth travel-reservation system that has been known to process over 250,000 reservations *in just one day*. Through a special computer connection known as a *gateway* between AOL and EAAsy Sabre, all the information and power of this reservation system can now be at your finger-tips. This page shows you how to get started.

## TIP SHEET

▶ From the Reservations Menu mentioned in step 5, you can also research and reserve hotel rooms and rental cars. Just enter the appropriate number: 3 for Hotels or 4 for Rental Cars.

▶ You can use EAAsy Sabre at any time to re-search travel arrangements, but before you can actually make any online reservations, you must first complete an online registration application. To do this, enter 5 on the EAAsy Sabre Main Menu, and then follow the on-screen instructions. Registration is free and immediate.

▶ EAAsy Sabre is not case sensitive. For exam-ple, even though EAAsy Sabre instructs you to type /EXIT to exit the system, you can also type /exit or /Exit to achieve the same results.

▶ Note the system navigation commands at the bottom of the EAAsy Sabre Main Menu shown in step 5. These commands are very useful if you get lost or need helpful informa-tion while working with EAAsy Sabre.

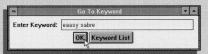

**1** Make sure you're signed on to AOL, and then use the keyword **eaasy sabre**, or **easy sabre**, or **sabre**. (Or click on the Toolbar's Travel & Shopping icon, and then click on Airline & Hotel Reservations.)

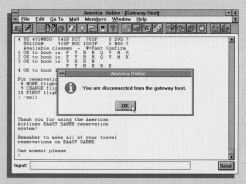

**8** When you're done using EAAsy Sabre, type **/exit** or **/e**, click on Send, click on OK to close the dialog box shown here, and then close the Gateway Host window to return to AOL.

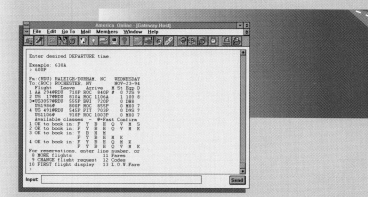

**7** Once you've answered all the applicable questions, EAAsy Sabre displays a list of scheduled flights that most closely match your travel plans. From here, you can compare fares, pick the flight that best fits your plans and budget, and research return flights. You can't actually make flight reservations until you reg-ister to use EAAsy Sabre (see the second Tip on this page), but you can always print out the flight infor-mation and give it to your travel agent.

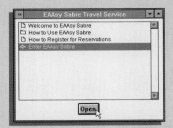

**2** The EAAsy Sabre Travel Service window opens. (Or, if you clicked on Airline & Hotel Reservations in step 1, you'll see a very similar Airline & Hotel Reservations window.) Click on Enter EAAsy Sabre, and then click on Open.

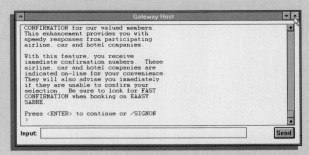

**3** A Gateway Host window opens. You have just passed through the EAAsy Sabre gateway, and your computer is now communicating directly with the EAAsy Sabre system. To make the text in this window easier to read, maximize the Gateway Host window.

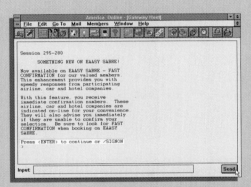

**4** Take your time, read each screen of text carefully, and you should find EAAsy Sabre fairly self-explanatory and easy to use. Each screen displays some information, and then provides instructions on what type of information it needs from you. This screen, for example, advises you to press Enter (an alternative to clicking on Send) or to enter /SIGNON (that is, to type **/SIGNON** and then press Enter or click on Send). The /SIGNON command is available only to people who have already registered to use EAAsy Sabre, so just click on Send or press Enter.

**6** EAAsy Sabre asks you step-by-step questions about your travel plans, including city of departure, city of arrival, preferred airports (if applicable), and preferred travel date and time. Type in your answers to each of the questions presented, and click on Send after each answer.

**5** After reading EAAsy Sabre's Terms and Conditions (something you should do *before* making any online reservations), you finally arrive at the EAAsy Sabre Main Menu. To start researching airline flights from here, type **2** for Reservations and Travel Information and click on Send to move to the Reservations Menu. Then type **1** for Flight Availability and click on Send.

# How to Use Travelers' Corner

Whether you've already made your travel plans or are still working on them, Travelers' Corner is a good place to learn more about any and all destinations. Developed and maintained by Weissmann Travel Reports, a major information provider to the travel industry, Travelers' Corner provides profiles on every state in the U.S. and on just about every country in the world. These concise, up-to-date profiles are alphabetically arranged so that you can quickly and easily find just the information you're seeking. This page shows you how to take a look at these profiles.

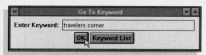

**1** Make sure you're signed on to AOL, and then use the keyword **travelers corner** or **weissmann**. (Or click on the Toolbar's Travel & Shopping icon, and then on Travelers' Corner.)

## TIP SHEET

▶ If you prefer, you can also search for destinations by clicking on Search in step 3 rather than on an alphabetical group. For best results, search by state for U.S. destinations, and by country for international destinations.

▶ The online reports you see here are abridged from more detailed reports that are available in print. To order a printed report that you have to pay for, click on Order Travel Reports in the Travelers' Corner window. To get a free copy instead, visit a travel agent that carries Weissmann Travel Reports.

▶ Travelers' Corner also provides an Exotic Destinations Message Center (message board), an online version of the award-winning *Travel Holiday* magazine, and more. Explore the Travelers' Corner window to see what's available.

▶ Besides Travelers' Corner, AOL offers another separate travel-oriented area, the Travel Forum. To visit this area, use the keyword *travel forum* or *traveler*.

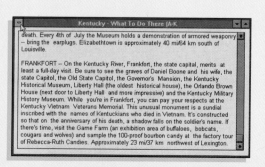

**6** When you're done reading (or saving or printing) an article, close the article's window, and then repeat step 5 as desired to read other articles.

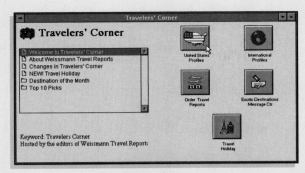

**2** To start looking for the profile of a U.S. destination, click on United States Profiles. To start looking for the profile of an international destination, click on International Profiles.

**3** If you clicked on United States Profiles in step 2, you'll see the U.S. Profiles window shown here. If you clicked on International Profiles, a similar International Profiles window opens. U.S. profiles are categorized by state; international profiles are categorized by country. To see a list of available states or countries, click the button for the appropriate alphabetical group.

**4** Another U.S. Profiles or International Profiles window opens. Scroll to find the desired state or country, and then double-click on it.

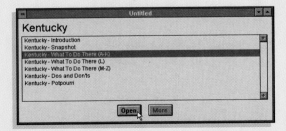

**5** State and country profiles are divided into five article types: Introduction, Snapshot, What to Do There, Dos and Don'ts, and Potpourri. Each article details a different aspect of the state or country. To read one of the articles, click on it and then click on Open.

## CHAPTER 14

# Online Shopping

 Few communities, even electronic ones, are complete without shopping opportunities—and AOL provides plenty of ways to shop on line.

You already know from Chapter 13 that you can reserve airline flights, hotel rooms, and rental cars on line, but these are only a fraction of the shopping opportunities available in AOL's Travel & Shopping department, a veritable mall of online stores.

Interested in discounts of 10 to 50 percent on over 250,000 brand name products? Look no further than Comp-u-Store. Time to stock up on office supplies? Penny Wise Office Products probably has just what you need—and at discount prices. For the latest in computer hardware or software, check out Computer Express, PC Catalog, or the Komando Mall. Have a big fight last night? Say "I'm sorry" with roses from the Flower Stop. AutoVantage Online helps you get the best possible price on a new car. And if you're just looking for a good old-fashioned book to read so that you can rest your screen-weary eyes, enjoy 10 to 20 percent savings at the Online Bookstore.

Maybe mall shopping isn't your thing. Maybe you just need some extra cash or you're seeking or offering employment. If so, look into Classifieds Online, AOL's main area for member-to-member advertising.

So grab your wallet—we're going shopping!

# How to Shop at an Online Store

**W**ith all the online stores that AOL has to offer, it's impossible to show them all on just one page. Instead, we've chosen to introduce you to one store that should interest every AOL member: the AOL Products Center. Here, you can buy AOL paraphernalia, to show off your community pride. Although every online store (unfortunately) works differently, this page will give you at least a taste of AOL online shopping.

**TIP SHEET**

▶ **To review and optionally delete an item from your electronic shopping cart before checking out, open the Your Shopping Cart dialog box shown in step 6, click on the item, and then on Review/Delete Item.**

▶ **If you leave the AOL Products Center before checking out, none of your selected items will be ordered. However, if you return to the Center before signing off from AOL, your electronic shopping cart will still contain those items, and you can easily pick up where you left off.**

▶ **Remember that shopping in other online stores will be different from shopping in the AOL Products Center. Some stores use an electronic shopping cart like the one shown here; others don't. Shopping in some stores is free, and others charge membership fees. Be patient, read each store's instructions, and you'll soon be an online shopping expert.**

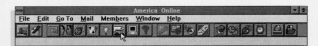

▶ **1** Make sure you're signed on to AOL, and then click on the Toolbar's Travel & Shopping icon. (Or use the keyword **shopping**.)

**8** A Credit Card Information window opens. Fill in the text boxes with your credit card number, expiration date, and name as it appears on the card, and then click on Continue. As shown here, use no spaces, dashes, or slashes in the credit card number or expiration date. Finally, click on OK to close the next dialog box, which confirms your order.

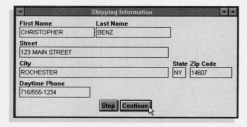

**7** A Shipping Information window opens, displaying the master-account holder's name, address, and telephone number as it exists in AOL's membership billing database. If you want your items shipped to this name and address, click on Continue. Otherwise, change the information as necessary, and then click on Continue.

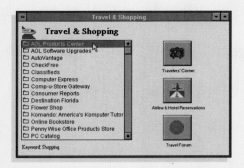

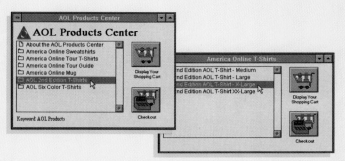

**2** The Travel & Shopping window opens, displaying a long list of on-line stores. Double-click on AOL Products Center.

**3** The AOL Products Center window opens, listing AOL sweat-shirts, T-shirts, and so on. Double-click on an item that inter-ests you. In the next window, double-click on the desired color, size, and/or version (as applicable) of your selected item.

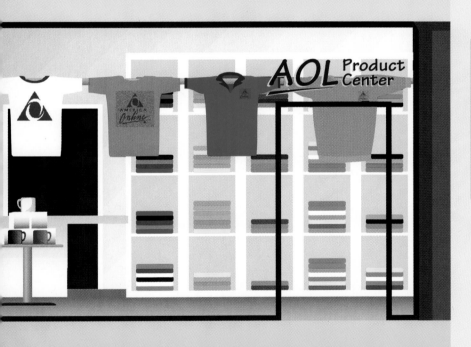

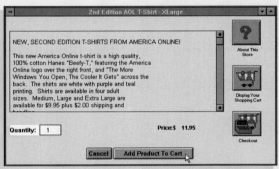

**4** The next window displays a description of your selected item and its cost, including shipping and handling. To add the current item to your *electronic shopping cart*, indi-cate the desired quantity in the Quantity text box (if you're ordering just one, you can leave this text box as is), and then click on Add Product To Cart. (If you *don't* want to order the current item, click on Cancel.)

**5** To order other items, return to the AOL Products Center window shown in step 3, and then repeat steps 3 and 4 as desired. When you've selected all the items you want, click on any Display Your Shopping Cart or Checkout button.

**6** The Your Shopping Cart dialog box opens, displaying the items in your elec-tronic shopping cart, and the total cost of those items. To start finalizing your order, click on Checkout.

# How to Use Classifieds Online

**D**o you pore through your newspaper's classi-fied ads, looking for good bargains on pre-enjoyed items? Do you have a garage, basement, or attic stuffed with possessions that you'll probably never use again, but that are just too valuable to throw or give away? Are you seeking a job or offering one? If you answered yes to any of these questions, then AOL's Classifieds Online area may be just the place for you. Classifieds Online comprises a set of AOL message boards (see Chapter 6) with the specific purpose of helping AOL members buy, sell, and trade old treasures and professional skills.

**TIP SHEET**

▶ **As with any classified ads, be careful when using them. Most AOL members are trust-worthy, but the occasional one might try to cheat you. Check out the Tradin' Talk board for recommended members and safe-trading tips. To access this board, double-click on Tradin' Talk (no ads) in the Classifieds Online window. (Trading tips are also available by clicking on the center button in this window.)**

▶ **One of the few rules in Classifieds Online is that you must post your ad to the correct board, *only* to that board, and only *once* on that board.**

▶ **Each night, every topic is trimmed down to the 300 most recent ads. This means that your ad may remain posted for only a day or so. Feel free to post your ad again once it's been removed.**

▶ **For convenient access to classified ads lo-cated elsewhere on AOL, double-click on Other classifieds in the Classifieds Online window.**

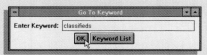

**1** Make sure you're signed on to AOL, and then use the keyword **classifieds**. (Or click on the Toolbar's Travel & Shopping icon, and then double-click on Classifieds.)

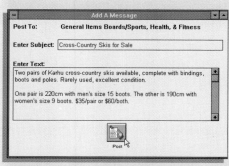

**8** Type up your ad, making sure that the subject and message are as specific and detailed as pos-sible, and then click on Post. Don't forget to check your e-mail frequently after posting an ad, to see if you've received any responses.

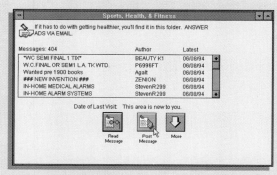

**7** To post an ad of your own, click on Post Message. (Or click on Add Message if you're already reading an ad.)

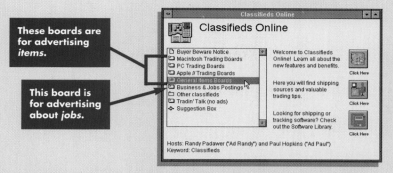

These boards are for advertising *items*.

This board is for advertising about *jobs*.

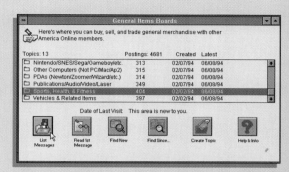

**2** The Classifieds Online window opens. If you want to buy, sell, or trade an *item*, double-click on the most appropriate list-box choice that contains the word *Boards*. If you're seeking or offering *employment*, double-click on Business & Job Postings, and then on Employment Offered or Wanted.

**3** The next window lists the topics contained within your chosen board. Scroll as necessary, click on the most appropriate topic, and then click on List Messages.

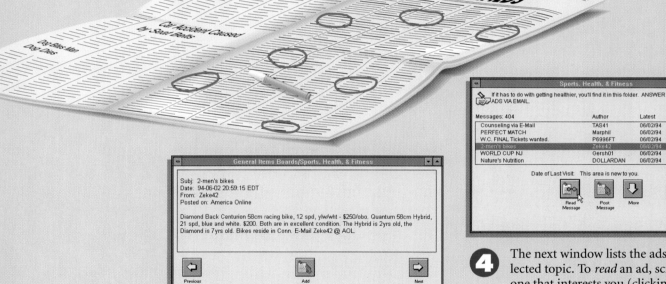

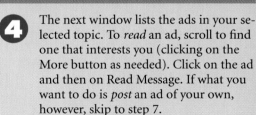

**4** The next window lists the ads in your selected topic. To *read* an ad, scroll to find one that interests you (clicking on the More button as needed). Click on the ad and then on Read Message. If what you want to do is *post* an ad of your own, however, skip to step 7.

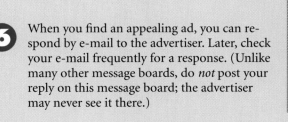

**5** The next window displays the ad you selected. Read the ad to see if it describes what you want. If it doesn't, close the window and repeat step 4 to continue reading ads. (Or use the Previous Message or Next Message buttons to move directly from one ad to another.)

**6** When you find an appealing ad, you can respond by e-mail to the advertiser. Later, check your e-mail frequently for a response. (Unlike many other message boards, do *not* post your reply on this message board; the advertiser may never see it there.)

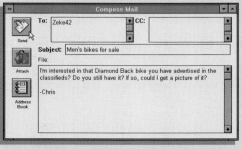

# CHAPTER 15

# Downloading Files

 In Chapter 7, you learned that you can download files that are attached to mail messages. But a bigger selection of files is also available to you online: AOL offers over 50,000 publicly available files—from games and graphics to diagnostic utilities and full-blown word processing programs. And except for your online charges, you can download any or all of these files for free!

You might question the legality of this. After all, it *is* illegal to upload or download copyrighted files without permission. Fortunately, both you and AOL already *have* this permission. Unlike the commercial software you might buy in a store, each of AOL's downloadable files are generally one of three special software types—freeware, shareware, or demoware—all of which can be uploaded, downloaded, or otherwise copied at will.

*Freeware* (also know as *public domain software*) is just what the name implies: software that's completely free. *Shareware* is software that you *try* for free, but for which you must pay a nominal fee (generally $2–$30) should you decide to use the software beyond the specified trial period. *Demoware* is generally a trimmed-down version of a larger commercial program, provided free as an enticement to buy the full-function version.

Regardless of price, much of this software is of surprisingly high quality that sometimes rivals or even surpasses its commercial counterparts. So take a chance, download a file or two, and see what no money can get you.

# How to Search for and Download a File

AOL's downloadable files are organized into specialized file collections called *software libraries*. Software libraries can be found in every AOL department—usually indicated by buttons or list-box items that display a stack of floppy disks—and provide a good way to browse topic-specific files. These libraries are, however, by their very nature limited in scope and can sometimes be difficult to find. Rather than trying to work with these individual libraries, you can get central access to most downloadable files through *File Search*, AOL's searchable database of files. This page shows you how to search for files, and how to download a file once you've found it.

**TIP SHEET**

▶ **Once you've downloaded a file, it's ready to use. If you're still relatively inexperienced with computers, ask a computer-savvy friend to show you how to locate and use this downloaded file. By default, the file will be found on your hard disk in the directory (a subsection of the disk) specified by the Download Manager window shown in step 5. This directory is usually c:\waol\download or c:\waol15\download.**

▶ **Don't be concerned if a file description indicates that you need an "UnZIPing" program. If the file ends with .ZIP or .ARC, AOL for Windows *is* your unZIPing program.**

▶ **If the file you're downloading contains a computer *image* (also known as a *picture* or *graphic*), step 6 may be slightly different. You might see an Image Transfer dialog box instead of the File Transfer dialog box, and you might see the image on screen as it downloads.**

▶ **Try using the keyword *software* to visit the Software Center, one of AOL's most popular file-library areas.**

▶ **1** Make sure you're signed on to AOL, and then click on the Toolbar's File Search icon. (Or use the keyword **file search** or **quickfind**.)

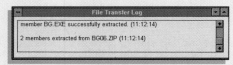

**8** When you're done using AOL, sign off without exiting AOL for Windows. (Choose Exit from the File menu, and then click on Yes.) If the file you downloaded ends with .ZIP or .ARC—indicating that the file is stored in a compressed format to save download time—the File Transfer Log window will open to show what file or files ("members") have been extracted from the compressed file.

**7** When the download is complete, a Download Manager dialog box opens to indicate this. Click on OK to close the dialog box.

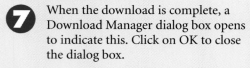

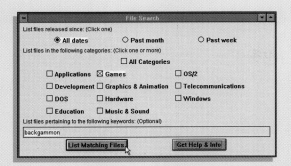

**2** The File Search window opens. To get a list of the newest files, click on Past month or Past week at the top of the window; otherwise, leave All dates selected. To narrow the search, check one or more specific categories. To narrow the search even further, type a search criterion or criteria at the bottom of the window. (For more information on using search criteria, see Chapter 9.) When you're ready, click on List Matching Files.

**3** After a moment, a File Search Results window opens, listing the files that meet your search parameters. Scroll to find a file that interests you (using the List More Files button when it's available, to add files to the list). When you see one of interest, click on the file and then on Read Description. If you can't find a file that interests you, return to the File Search window and repeat step 2.

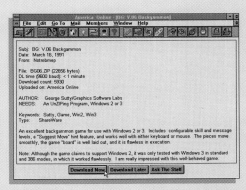

**4** A detailed description of the selected file opens (you can maximize the description window as shown here, if desired). Read the description carefully. Pay close attention to the estimated time it will take to download the file, the computer equipment and/or software necessary to use the file, and the general description. If you want to download this file, click on Download Now. Otherwise, return to the File Search Results window and repeat step 3.

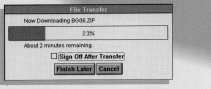

**5** A Download Manager window opens, giving you the option to specify a different file name or disk location for the file. For now, just click on OK.

**6** A File Transfer dialog box opens, displaying the progress of your file transfer (download).

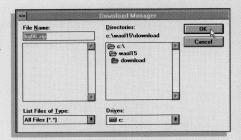

# How to Use the Download Manager

O n the previous page, you learned how to download a single file. But what if you want to download more than one file at a time, or what if you don't want to start downloading files until after you've completed some other AOL exploration? In either case, you can call upon AOL's Download Manager to help. The Download Manager is essentially a to-do list, keeping track of every file you've decided to download. As you perform multiple file searches and/or explore multiple software libraries, you simply add files to the list. Then, when you're ready to download, you ask the Download Manager to download every selected file, all at once. This page shows you how.

**TIP SHEET**

▶ **Once you've signed off from AOL, the Download Manager can still serve several purposes. Click on the Toolbar's Download Manager icon or choose Download Manager from the File menu to see a list of files that you've selected for downloading, but haven't yet downloaded. Click on Show Files Downloaded at this point, and you'll open a Files You've Downloaded list.**

▶ **If you accidentally sign off and exit AOL for Windows in one step after downloading a compressed file, AOL for Windows will *not* automatically decompress that file. To decompress this file manually, open the Files You've Downloaded list as described in the previous tip, click on the compressed file, and then click on Decompress.**

▶ **For lengthy downloads, check Sign Off After Transfer in step 5, and then turn your attention to other matters. AOL for Windows will then automatically download your files, sign off, and extract files as appropriate.**

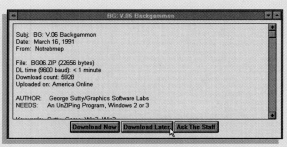

▶ **1** Once you've used File Search or a software library to locate and display the description of a file that you want to download, click on Download Later rather than on Download Now.

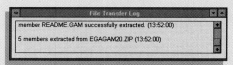

**7** When you're done using AOL, sign off without exiting AOL for Windows. If any of the files you downloaded end with .ZIP or .ARC, the File Transfer Log window will show what file or files have been extracted from those compressed files. Your downloaded files are now ready to use.

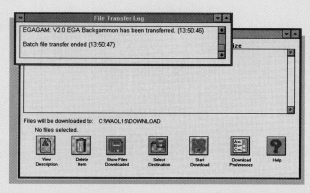

**6** When the download is complete, the File Transfer dialog box closes automatically; the File Transfer Log and Download Manager windows remain open.

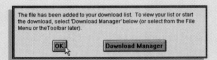

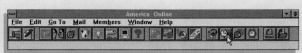

**2** A dialog box informs you that the selected file has been added to your download list. Click on OK to close this dialog box.

**3** Repeat steps 1 and 2 for each file that you want to download. Feel free to explore AOL between adding files to your download list. When you're finally ready to start the download, click on the Toolbar's Download Manager icon, or choose Download Manager from the File menu. (If you're ready to download immediately after adding the last file to your list, you can also click on Download Manager rather than on OK in step 2.)

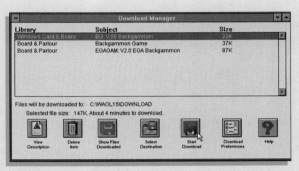

**4** A Download Manager window opens, listing the files you've selected. Click on Start Download.

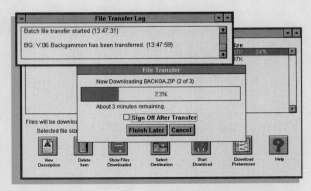

**5** Next you'll see a File Transfer dialog box and a File Transfer Log window. The File Transfer dialog box displays the progress of your overall download, while the File Transfer Log window displays a download log. In the Download Manager window in the background, you may also be able to see the progress of each file as it's downloaded.

# TRY IT!

**H**ere's a hands-on opportunity to practice some of the many techniques involved in searching for and downloading files. In this exercise, you'll use many of the techniques you've read about in Chapter 15, as well as some important techniques from earlier chapters. Chapter numbers are included in parentheses at the end of each step to show you where we first introduced the technique required to perform that step. (**Note:** Before attempting this activity, be sure that you have installed AOL for Windows and have set up your AOL membership account. For details, see Chapter 3.)

**1**

If necessary, switch on your computer and start Windows (Chapter 2).

Open the America Online program group, and then double-click on the America Online program item to start AOL for Windows (Chapter 3).

Verify that *your* screen name (*not* the one shown here) is displayed in the Screen Name dropdown list box, and then type your password in the Password text box (Chapter 3).

Click on Sign On (Chapter 3).

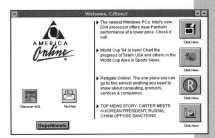

Wait a few moments as AOL for Windows dials your local access number, connects to AOL, checks your password, and then opens the online Welcome! window (Chapter 3).

Click on the Toolbar's File Search icon, or use the keyword **file search** (Chapter 15).

In the File Search window, check Windows, type **speaker driver**, and then click on List Matching Files (Chapter 15).

In the File Search Results window, click on the file item that ends with SPEAK.EXE, and then click on Read Description (Chapter 15).

Continue to next page ▶

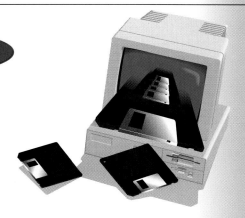

**TRY IT!**

Continue
below

**12**

In the File
Search win-
dow, check
Windows,
type **screen
savers and magic**, and then click on
List Matching Files (Chapter 15).

**9**

Maximize the
description
window, read
the file de-
scription,
and then
click on
Download
Later (Chapters 2 and 15).

**13**

In the File
Search
Results win-
dow, click on
the file item that ends with MAGIC1.ZIP, if
necessary, and then click on Read Description
(Chapter 15).

**10**

The file has been added to your download list. To view your list or start
the download, select 'Download Manager' below (or select from the File
Menu or the Toolbar later).

OK        Download Manager

Click on OK
to close this
dialog box (Chapter 15).

**14**

Maximize the
description
window, read
the file
description,
and then
click on
Download
Later (Chapters 2 and 15).

**11**

Click again on the Toolbar's File Search
icon (Chapter 15).

**15**

The file has been added to your download list. To view your list or start
the download, select 'Download Manager' below (or select from the File
Menu or the Toolbar later).

OK        Download Manager

Click on
Download
Manager in this dialog box (Chapter 15).

**16** In the Download Manager window, click on Start Download (Chapter 15).

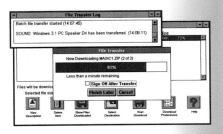

**17** Wait a few minutes (depending on the speed of your modem) as the Download Manager downloads the two files (Chapter 15).

**18** When the File Transfer dialog box closes, the download is complete. Choose Exit from the File menu (Chapter 3).

**19** Click on Yes to sign off from AOL without exiting AOL for Windows (Chapter 3).

**20** Wait a few moments while AOL for Windows extracts files from MAGIC1.ZIP. When it's done, maximize the File Transfer Log window. This window should show that two files were downloaded, and that four members (files) were extracted from MAGIC1.ZIP (Chapters 2 and 15).

**21** Choose Exit from the File menu to close AOL for Windows (Chapter 3).

**22** Consulting with a computer-savvy friend as necessary, check out the files you just downloaded. SPEAK.EXE enables you to play sounds through your computer's built-in speaker in case you don't have a special sound board for this purpose. MAGIC1.ZIP is a customizable screensaver for Windows that draws colorful patterns on your computer monitor.

# CHAPTER 16

# Accessing the Internet

Relatively unknown until recently, *the Internet* has become a household phrase.

Often cited as a model for the U.S. government's proposed "national information superhighway," the Internet is the world's largest interconnection, or *network*, of computers. Originally created by the U.S. government in the late 1960s for sharing information between research scientists and military personnel nationwide, the Internet has since grown exponentially. It now includes connections to research facilities, military installations, government offices, educational institutions, businesses, and online services worldwide. Through these connections, an estimated 15 million people currently enjoy Internet access.

Although vast, widespread, and full of valuable information, the Internet suffers two major drawbacks: It can be difficult to connect to and even more difficult to use. Unlike AOL and other online services, the Internet was designed not for the average computer user, but for the most computer literate. Increasing the confusion is the fact that no one actually *owns* the Internet, making it next to impossible to redesign the system for easier use.

Fortunately, AOL is working diligently to improve its easy-to-use connection to the Internet, called AOL's Internet Center. Although the Internet is much too large and complex to cover in this one chapter, we will introduce you to two of its most popular features: newsgroups and mailing lists. (You already learned about the Internet's most popular feature, e-mail, in Chapter 7.)

# How to Read a Newsgroup

**N**ewsgroups—also known as *USENET groups, USENET news, Internet news,* and variations thereof—are the Internet's equivalent of AOL message boards (see Chapter 6), but on a worldwide scale. They contain online discussions rather than news. There are thousands upon thousands of available newsgroups, on topics ranging from dogs to volleyball to analyzing stock-market trends. With all these choices, it may seem an overwhelming task just to get started with newsgroups. For this reason, AOL already has set up a select list of newsgroups for you. On this page, you'll learn how to read one of these newsgroups.

▶ **1** Make sure you're signed on to AOL, and then use the keyword **newsgroups**. (Or use the keyword **internet** to open the Internet Center window, and then click on Newsgroups.)

### TIP SHEET

▶ Unlike AOL message boards, newsgroups track the messages you have and have not read, rather than the date you last visited a group. By clicking on List Unread Subjects (as shown in step 3) when you visit a group, you'll see only unread messages. To review messages you've already read, click instead on List All Subjects.

▶ To find out if a particular newsgroup is local or shared across the Internet, open the newsgroup as shown in step 3, and examine the newsgroup window's title bar. A local group's title bar will contain the phrase "[Local Only]."

▶ AOL's local newsgroups contain important information about the accepted conventions, known as *Netiquette,* for posting messages to newsgroups. Once you're familiar with these rules of Netiquette, try posting your own message. To do so, click on a Send New Message or Send Response button from anywhere within the newsgroup subject to which you want to post.

 To jump directly to another subject within the current newsgroup, return to the group's subject window, click on the desired subject, and then on Read Messages or List Messages. To start reading another newsgroup, return to the Read My Newsgroups window, click on the desired group, and then on List Unread Subjects.

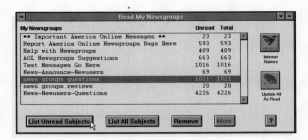

**2** The Newsgroups window opens. Click on Read My Newsgroups. If a window entitled Newsgroups MOTD (Message of the Day) opens next, read the message, and then click on OK to close the window.

**3** The Read My Newsgroups window opens, listing the newsgroups that AOL has set up for you, and the number of total and unread messages contained within each group. The newsgroups toward the top of this list are "local," shared only among AOL members, and have been created by AOL to help you learn about newsgroups. The remainder are true Internet newsgroups, shared across the Internet. Click on any one of these groups, and then on List Unread Subjects.

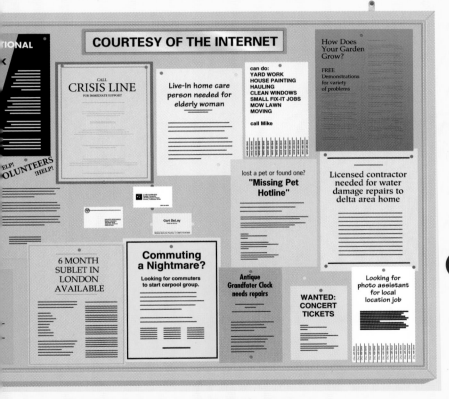

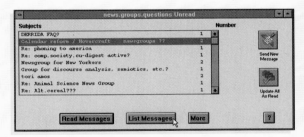

**4** Another window opens, listing your chosen newsgroup's subjects and the number of messages contained within each subject. Click on a subject, and then click on List Messages. (To save a step and proceed directly to the selected subject's first message, you can click on Read Messages instead, and then skip to step 6.)

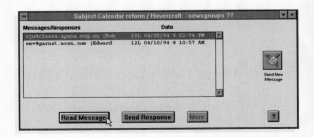

**5** The next window you see lists your chosen subject's messages. Each listing contains the message sender's Internet address, and the date and time the message was posted. Click on a message, and then click on Read Message.

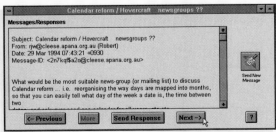

**6** Another window opens, displaying your chosen message. When you've finished reading this message, click on Next to display the next message in your chosen category. Or, if you've already reached the current subject's last message, clicking on Next will display the first message in the *next* subject.

# How to Add a Newsgroup

Once you've read through the newsgroups that AOL has set up for you, you might want to start tapping into newsgroups that focus on particular topics that interest you, whether it be international politics or wine making. To facilitate this, you customize your Read My Newsgroups list by adding news-groups to the list. Once you've added a news-group to this list, reading the group and posting messages to it are the same as for any of the newsgroups in your existing list. This page shows you how to add a newsgroup to your newsgroups list.

**TIP SHEET**

▶ To review a newsgroup before adding it to your newsgroups list, click on List Subjects or Read Messages in step 5 *before* using the Add button.

▶ The Newsgroups window shown in step 1 provides three additional ways to add newsgroups to your list. If you know the exact Internet name for a newsgroup (per-haps you've read about it in another group), you can use the Expert Add button. To see the newest available newsgroups, click on Latest Newsgroups. To search for news-groups, click on Search All Newsgroups.

▶ Be aware that Internet newsgroups are *not* subject to AOL's family-oriented terms of ser-vice, and might contain subject matter and language not suitable for everyone.

▶ To remove a newsgroup from your news-groups list, click on the group in your Read My Newsgroups window, click on Remove, and then click on OK in each of the two dia-log boxes that follow.

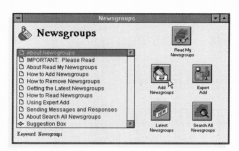

▶ **1** Open the Newsgroups window as described in step 1 on the previous page, and then click on Add Newsgroups.

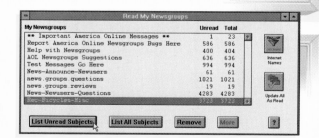

**7** Now when you open your Read My Newsgroups window, your newly added newsgroup appears in the list. (This group might be displayed with a somewhat different name than what you clicked on in step 4.) You can now use the techniques de-scribed on the previous page to read and post messages in this group.

**2** The Add Newsgroups - Categories window opens, listing the many available newsgroup categories and the number of topics contained within each category. Click on one of these categories, and then on List Topics.

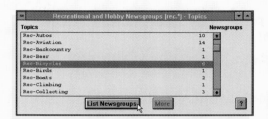

**3** The next window lists your chosen category's topics and the number of available newsgroups within each topic. Click on a topic, and then on List Newsgroups.

**4** The next window lists your chosen topic's newsgroups and the number of messages within each group. If you see a newsgroup that you want to add to your customized list, click on that group, and then on Add.

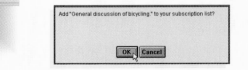

**5** A dialog box opens to ask if you want to add this group to your newsgroups list. Click on OK to confirm your request.

**6** If all goes well, a second dialog box opens to inform you that your request to add the group has been accepted. Click on OK to close this dialog box.

# How to Search for and Subscribe to a Mailing List

Like newsgroups, Internet *mailing lists* are topic-specific online discussion groups. The chief difference between newsgroups and mailing lists is how you gain access to these discussions. Rather than maintaining lists of messages, a mailing list exchanges messages through e-mail. To become part of a mailing list, you send e-mail to a specific e-mail address, requesting a *subscription* to that list. Within a few days, you'll start receiving in your AOL mailbox any messages that are sent to that mailing list. Once you become familiar with a particular mailing list, you, too, can start sending messages to everyone on that list.

**TIP SHEET**

▶ One of the drawbacks of subscribing to a mailing list is the 550-message limit in all your AOL mailboxes at any one time. Once you've reached 550, AOL automatically starts removing older messages. Although 550 may seem like a lot, some mailing lists can generate hundreds of messages *per day*. If you subscribe to one or more lists, check your mail regularly.

▶ If a mailing list generates more messages than you can handle, you might want to *unsubscribe* from the list. To do this, follow the instructions you got in step 4 or in step 6.

▶ Be aware that, like newsgroups, mailing lists might contain subject matter and language not suitable for everyone.

▶ This chapter has shown you two of the Internet's many resources. To learn how to tap into a vast collection of online databases, transfer files to and from the Internet, and even take remote control of other computers, explore AOL's Internet Center by using the keyword *internet*.

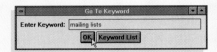

▶ **1** Make sure you're signed on to AOL, and then use the keyword **mailing lists**. (Or use the keyword **internet** to open the Internet Center window, and then click on Mailing Lists.)

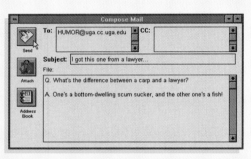

**8** After reading enough messages to get a good feel for the topic, try sending your own message to the mailing list, by following the instructions you got in step 4 or have since received from the list.

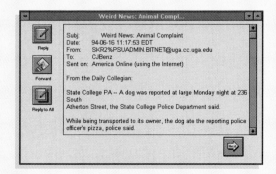

**7** Shortly thereafter, depending on the list's popularity, you should start receiving messages from other list members. Here is an example.

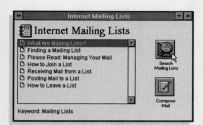

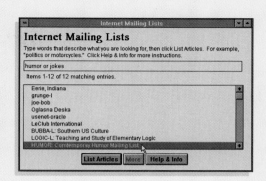

**2** The Internet Mailing Lists window opens. Click on Search Mailing Lists.

**3** The Internet Mailing Lists search window opens. Use the techniques you learned in Chapter 9 to type in search criteria. Then click on List Articles to display mailing lists that meet your criteria, and double-click on one of these lists.

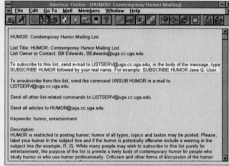

**4** The next window that opens displays a description of your chosen mailing list, along with specific instructions for becoming part of that list. We maximized the window shown here so that you can see it better, but you should print your window's contents for reference.

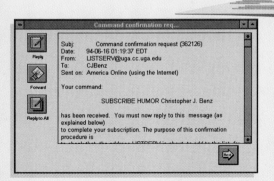

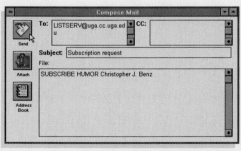

**6** Every mailing list is different, but for most lists, you should receive fairly soon an e-mail message about your subscription request. If this message asks you to confirm your subscription, carefully follow the instructions for doing so. You may receive additional messages with instructions for appropriate message content, where to send messages, and so on.

**5** To subscribe now to the mailing list you have displayed, compose and send an e-mail message, carefully following the subscription instructions from step 4. If your chosen list is maintained by a *list server* (an automated program that maintains the list), the instructions will tell you to type a short, specific command in the body of your message. If no command is specified, assume that your message is going to an actual person, and send a politely worded subscription request. (If you need help with e-mail, review Chapter 7.)

# APPENDIX

# Goodbye!

 Congratulations! Having read this far, you now should be a comfortable, confident AOL member, ready to find online information with a minimum of effort, time, and expense. We hope that this book will continue to serve as a handy reference guide for all your future AOL explorations.

As a reward for your accomplishment, we're leaving you with a gift: some bonus tips that will help you use AOL and AOL for Windows even more efficiently.

Read on and learn.

## Bonus Tips

As we produced this book, we came up with several useful tips that really didn't fit anywhere else in the book. Many of those tips are listed here. Although these suggestions certainly aren't crucial to your success in using AOL, they can save you some effort, aggravation, and online time, as well as help you make AOL work the way *you* want it to.

**1. Escape from the hourglass.** When you open an online window, it can take from several seconds to several minutes for that window's information to travel from AOL to your computer. In the meantime, your mouse pointer changes to an hourglass, indicating that you should wait. In most cases, the hourglass will disappear immediately, indicating that you can now close this window and continue on to other tasks. But if the window's information isn't something you're interested in anyway and you don't want to wait, you can stop the information flow by pressing the Escape key or by choosing Stop Incoming Text from the File menu. If the window contains information that you do want to read, you can go ahead and start scrolling while the hourglass is still visible.

**2. Log text.** Rather than reading text on line, or manually saving or printing text from individual online windows, you can instead automatically capture, or *log*, the text from *every* window you open. This text moves directly into a disk file, which you can then open and read after you sign off. To learn more about the File, Logging command, consult offline help. (See Chapter 10 for information on using offline help.)

**3. Working with text you've saved.** Once you've saved or logged text to a disk, you can view, edit, and even print that text from within AOL for Windows. To do this, choose Open from the File menu, click on the file's name, and then click on OK. Text that you've saved to disk can also be opened with many other Windows applications, including Notepad, Write, and many popular word processing programs.

**4. Working with a downloaded image.** Besides viewing an image as you download it, you can also redisplay that image within AOL for Windows (version 1.5 only). To do so, use the File, Open command as described in the previous tip. You can also view many downloaded images using some other Windows applications, including Paintbrush and most word processing programs.

**5. Use the Windows Clipboard.** The Windows Clipboard enables you to transfer text quickly and easily from one AOL window to another, from AOL for Windows to other Windows applications, and from other Windows applications to AOL for Windows. You can use the Clipboard for thousands of purposes—from copying a complex e-mail address to using a word processing program for spell-checking your outgoing mail messages. To use the Clipboard, select (drag across) the text you want to transfer, choose either Cut or Copy from the Edit menu, position the insertion point wherever you want to place the text, and then choose Paste from the File menu. To learn more about the Windows Clipboard, consult your Windows documentation.

**6. Create your own window.** Choose New from the File menu to open a blank window in which you can type text. You can save quite a bit of online time by typing text in one of these windows when you're off line, and then using the Clipboard to transfer the text to an online window.

**7. Avoid AOL when it's slow.** As you've worked with AOL, you may have discovered that the service works very quickly at some times, and very slowly at others. This is affected by how many members are signed on to AOL at the time: the more members on line, the slower the system. To save yourself some online charges, especially when you're downloading files, avoid AOL during its peak times of evenings and weekends.

**8. Accept that some windows just don't close.** You may have discovered that some online windows, such as the online Welcome! window, never actually close. You can *minimize* the window, or you can *hide* it by entering a free area, but you can't close it. Don't waste your time worrying about it.

**9. Set your preferences.** Use the Members, Preferences command to change the way AOL for Windows works overall. For example, you can tell AOL for Windows to automatically scroll windows as they fill with text, and you can have AOL for Windows automatically notify you when a member enters or leaves your current chat room. To learn more about setting preferences, consult offline help.

**10. Explore Members Helping Members.** For hundreds of additional AOL tips from fellow members, take some time to peruse the Members Helping Members message board. Click on Member to Member in Your Online Help Center (see Chapter 10), or use the keyword *mhm*. If you have a valuable tip of your own, be sure to post it on this board so that other members can benefit from it.

# INDEX

# Imagination.
# Innovation. Insight.

## The How It Works Series from Ziff-Davis Press

"... a magnificently seamless integration of text and graphics ..."

Larry Blasko, The Associated Press, reviewing *PC/Computing How Computers Work*

No other books bring computer technology to life like the *How It Works* series from Ziff-Davis Press. Lavish, full-color illustrations and lucid text from some of the world's top computer commentators make *How It Works* books an exciting way to explore the inner workings of PC technology.

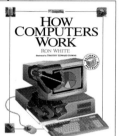

ISBN: 094-7 Price: $22.95

### PC/Computing How Computers Work

A worldwide blockbuster that hit the general trade bestseller lists! *PC/Computing* magazine executive editor Ron White dismantles the PC and reveals what really makes it tick.

### How Networks Work

Two of the most respected names in connectivity showcase the PC network, illustrating and explaining how each component does its magic and how they all fit together.

ISBN: 129-3 Price: $24.95

### How Macs Work

A fun and fascinating voyage to the heart of the Macintosh! Two noted *MacUser* contributors cover the spectrum of Macintosh operations from startup to shutdown.

### How Software Works

This dazzlingly illustrated volume from Ron White peeks inside the PC to show in full-color how software breathes life into the PC. Covers Windows™ and all major software categories.

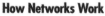

ISBN: 184-6 Price: $17.95

ISBN: 146-3 Price: $24.95

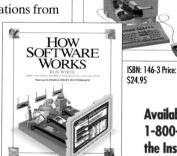

ISBN: 133-1 Price: $24.95

### How to Use Your Computer

Conquer computerphobia and see how this intricate machine truly makes life easier. Dozens of full-color graphics showcase the components of the PC and explain how to interact with them.

### All About Computers

This one-of-a-kind visual guide for kids features numerous full-color illustrations and photos on every page, combined with dozens of interactive projects that reinforce computer basics, making this an exciting way to learn all about the world of computers.

### How To Use Word

Make Word 6.0 for Windows Work for You!

A uniquely visual approach puts the basics of Microsoft's latest Windows-based word processor right before the reader's eyes. Colorful examples invite them to begin producing a variety of documents, quickly and easily. Truly innovative!

### How To Use Excel

Make Excel 5.0 for Windows Work for You!

Covering the latest version of Excel, this visually impressive resource guides beginners to spreadsheet fluency through a full-color graphical approach that makes powerful techniques seem plain as day. Hands-on "Try It" sections give new users a chance to sharpen newfound skills.

ISBN: 155-2 Price: $22.95

ISBN: 166-8 Price: $15.95

ISBN: 185-4 Price: $17.95

**Available at all fine bookstores or by calling 1-800-688-0448, ext. 100. Call for more information on the Instructor's Supplement, including transparencies for each book in the *How It Works* Series.**

ZIFF-DAVIS
ZD PRESS

© 1993 Ziff-Davis Press

# ATTENTION TEACHERS AND TRAINERS
# Now You Can Teach From These Books!

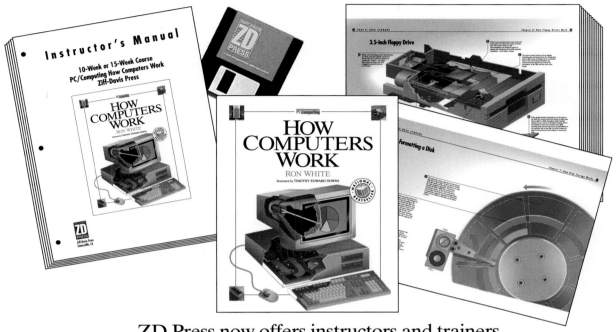

ZD Press now offers instructors and trainers
the materials they need to use these books in their classes.

- An Instructor's Manual features flexible lessons designed for use in a 10- or 15-week course (30-45 course hours).

- Student exercises and tests on floppy disk provide you with an easy way to tailor and/or duplicate tests as you need them.

- A Transparency Package contains all the graphics from the book, each on a single, full-color transparency.

- Spanish edition of *PC/Computing How Computers Work* will be available.

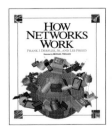

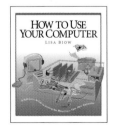
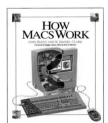

ZIFF-DAVIS ZD PRESS

# Your Road Map For The Information Superhighway— America Online®

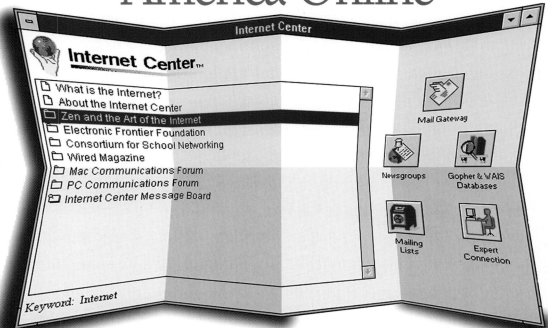

*See other side for details about your FREE trial of America Online!*

# Test Drive The Internet On America Online For 10 Hours, FREE.

## The Internet Center: More Content, Less Confusing.

America Online's Internet Center combines the easiest navigation with the most comprehensive collection of Internet resources of all the major online services.

- Internet e-mail with no surcharges
- Widest variety of university, corporate, and regional Newsgroups
- Over two months' worth of Newsgroup archives
- Best Gopher and WAIS sites organized for easy access
- Improved reliability due to extensive Gopher caching
- Available at 2400 baud, 9600 baud, and now over TCP/IP—all at one price
- More USENET Newsgroups than any other service—over 11,000, including the entire **alt.*** groups
- All Internet Gopher and WAIS databases, including fastest Veronica server, and it's *always* available

## Plus, hundreds of other features on America Online, including:

- NBC Online
- Unlimited e-mail
- The New York Times Online
- Stock and mutual fund quotes

- Live conferences and events
- Over 100,000 downloadable files
- DC Comics Online

## Clip and mail this card to:

AMERICA® *Online*

8619 Westwood Center Drive
Vienna, VA 22182-9806

Just clip and mail the attached card or fax it to us at 1-800-827-4595. Or simply call 1-800-827-6364, Ext. 4085.

Cut Here

Cut Here

# Ziff-Davis Press Survey of Readers

Please help us in our effort to produce the best books on personal computing.
For your assistance, we would be pleased to send you a FREE catalog
featuring the complete line of Ziff-Davis Press books.

### 1. How did you first learn about this book?

Recommended by a friend . . . . . . . . . . . . . . . ☐ -1 (5)
Recommended by store personnel . . . . . . . . . ☐ -2
Saw in Ziff-Davis Press catalog . . . . . . . . . . . ☐ -3
Received advertisement in the mail . . . . . . . . ☐ -4
Saw the book on bookshelf at store . . . . . . . . ☐ -5
Read book review in: _____ ☐ -6
Saw an advertisement in: _____ ☐ -7
Other (Please specify): _____ ☐ -8

### 2. Which THREE of the following factors most influenced your decision to purchase this book? (Please check up to THREE.)

Front or back cover information on book . . . ☐ -1 (6)
Logo of magazine affiliated with book . . . . . . ☐ -2
Special approach to the content . . . . . . . . . . ☐ -3
Completeness of content . . . . . . . . . . . . . . . . ☐ -4
Author's reputation. . . . . . . . . . . . . . . . . . . . ☐ -5
Publisher's reputation . . . . . . . . . . . . . . . . . ☐ -6
Book cover design or layout . . . . . . . . . . . . . ☐ -7
Index or table of contents of book . . . . . . . . ☐ -8
Price of book . . . . . . . . . . . . . . . . . . . . . . . . ☐ -9
Special effects, graphics, illustrations . . . . . . ☐ -0
Other (Please specify): _____ ☐ -x

### 3. How many computer books have you purchased in the last six months? _____ (7-10)

### 4. On a scale of 1 to 5, where 5 is excellent, 4 is above average, 3 is average, 2 is below average, and 1 is poor, please rate each of the following aspects of this book below. (Please circle your answer.)

Depth/completeness of coverage     5  4  3  2  1   (11)
Organization of material           5  4  3  2  1   (12)
Ease of finding topic              5  4  3  2  1   (13)
Special features/time saving tips  5  4  3  2  1   (14)
Appropriate level of writing       5  4  3  2  1   (15)
Usefulness of table of contents    5  4  3  2  1   (16)
Usefulness of index                5  4  3  2  1   (17)
Usefulness of accompanying disk    5  4  3  2  1   (18)
Usefulness of illustrations/graphics 5 4 3 2 1   (19)
Cover design and attractiveness    5  4  3  2  1   (20)
Overall design and layout of book  5  4  3  2  1   (21)
Overall satisfaction with book     5  4  3  2  1   (22)

### 5. Which of the following computer publications do you read regularly; that is, 3 out of 4 issues?

Byte . . . . . . . . . . . . . . . . . . . . . . . . . . . . . ☐ -1 (23)
Computer Shopper . . . . . . . . . . . . . . . . . . . ☐ -2
Corporate Computing . . . . . . . . . . . . . . . . . ☐ -3
Dr. Dobb's Journal . . . . . . . . . . . . . . . . . . . ☐ -4
LAN Magazine . . . . . . . . . . . . . . . . . . . . . . ☐ -5
MacWEEK . . . . . . . . . . . . . . . . . . . . . . . . . ☐ -6
MacUser . . . . . . . . . . . . . . . . . . . . . . . . . . ☐ -7
PC Computing . . . . . . . . . . . . . . . . . . . . . . ☐ -8
PC Magazine . . . . . . . . . . . . . . . . . . . . . . . ☐ -9
PC WEEK . . . . . . . . . . . . . . . . . . . . . . . . . ☐ -0
Windows Sources . . . . . . . . . . . . . . . . . . . . ☐ -x
Other (Please specify): _____ ☐ -y

**Please turn page.**

eo ƎɹAↃ ⌝⅃A⊥2 ⊥OᴎↃ—ᴛᴙƎᴙƎ ƎꓯA⊥

PLEASE TAPE HERE ONLY—DO NOT STAPLE

*Cut Here*

*Cut Here*

6. What is your level of experience with personal computers? With the subject of this book?

| | With PCs | With subject of book |
|---|---|---|
| Beginner. . . . . . . . . . . . . . | ☐ -1 (24) | ☐ -1 (25) |
| Intermediate. . . . . . . . . . | ☐ -2 | ☐ -2 |
| Advanced. . . . . . . . . . . . . | ☐ -3 | ☐ -3 |

7. Which of the following best describes your job title?

Officer (CEO/President/VP/owner). . . . . . . . ☐ -1 (26)
Director/head. . . . . . . . . . . . . . . . . . . . . . . ☐ -2
Manager/supervisor. . . . . . . . . . . . . . . . . . . ☐ -3
Administration/staff. . . . . . . . . . . . . . . . . . . ☐ -4
Teacher/educator/trainer. . . . . . . . . . . . . . . ☐ -5
Lawyer/doctor/medical professional. . . . . . . ☐ -6
Engineer/technician. . . . . . . . . . . . . . . . . . . ☐ -7
Consultant. . . . . . . . . . . . . . . . . . . . . . . . . . ☐ -8
Not employed/student/retired. . . . . . . . . . . . ☐ -9
Other (Please specify): _____ ☐ -0

8. What is your age?

Under 20. . . . . . . . . . . . . . . . . . . . . . . . . . . ☐ -1 (27)
21-29. . . . . . . . . . . . . . . . . . . . . . . . . . . . . . ☐ -2
30-39. . . . . . . . . . . . . . . . . . . . . . . . . . . . . . ☐ -3
40-49. . . . . . . . . . . . . . . . . . . . . . . . . . . . . . ☐ -4
50-59. . . . . . . . . . . . . . . . . . . . . . . . . . . . . . ☐ -5
60 or over. . . . . . . . . . . . . . . . . . . . . . . . . . ☐ -6

9. Are you:

Male. . . . . . . . . . . . . . . . . . . . . . . . . . . . . . . ☐ -1 (28)
Female. . . . . . . . . . . . . . . . . . . . . . . . . . . . . ☐ -2

Thank you for your assistance with this important information! Please write your address below to receive our free catalog.

Name: _____

Address: _____

City/State/Zip: _____

**Fold here to mail.**

2583-07-14

_____

_____

_____

**BUSINESS REPLY MAIL**
FIRST CLASS MAIL       PERMIT NO. 1612       OAKLAND, CA

POSTAGE WILL BE PAID BY ADDRESSEE

NO POSTAGE
NECESSARY
IF MAILED IN
THE UNITED
STATES

**Ziff-Davis Press**
5903 Christie Avenue
Emeryville, CA 94608-1925
Attn: Marketing